CHANGED LIVES

Ten True Stories: *From Addiction to Freedom*

compiled by
PASCO A. MANZO

FOREWORD BY DON WILKERSON

D0166638

Changed Lives
Ten True Stories: From Addiction to Freedom
Compiled by Pasco A. Manzo

Edited by Josiah D. Manzo
Cover Design by James Penswick
Layout Design by Justin Palojarvi
Photos by Colton Simmons

ISBN: 978-0-692-26145-3

Printed in the United States of America
2014 - Revised Edition

Dedication

"I dedicate this book to anyone suffering through addiction. Both those who have found FREEDOM through Jesus Christ and those who are still struggling with addiction. My wish is that through these pages you will find HOPE and a CHANGED LIFE according to His power that is continually at work within us."

Ephesians 3:20

Contents

Back Pages

Foreword

Don Wilkerson

At a time when drug abuse and addiction still plagues our society here are true life stories of modern day "miracles." I say miracles in the truest sense of the word. The ten people you will read about in Changed Lives have had an encounter with the highest power of THE Higher Power Jesus Christ, and they have never been the same.

Do you or someone you know need to be cured of addiction? Quickly put this book in their hands.

I highly recommend Changed Lives; each story will grip and inspire you.

As we say at and about Teen Challenge...

Hope lives here. Freedom is found here.
Changed lives leave here.

Introduction
The Drug Epidemic

Jacqui Strothoff

When I started to shoot heroin in 1967, most of the addicts were male, minorities from the inner-city who began shooting heroin as their first drug of choice. As a young, white, female from the suburbs who worked and ran the streets, I was quite an anomaly. Heroin was not the first drug I chose. My drug career progressed from cigarettes at age 10, to alcohol and pills at 12, then pot at 15, followed by heroin as a 17 year old.

In the 1950's illicit drug use was very popular within the "beatnik culture." It was often viewed as a way to enhance creativity of the artists and musicians of that time. It was the beginning of the "hippie generation" in the 1960's and their feel good philosophy of free love. Drug use was integral to their lifestyle, as it reflected a non-conformist attitude and ingesting hallucinogens also helped to expand their consciousness.

Changed Lives

This trend continued into the 1970's as recreational drug use was becoming more common. This was aided by the increase of cocaine availability, but heroin was also becoming more popular. In the 1980's a new and deadlier form of cocaine was introduced known as "crack" (because of the crackling sound it made when you smoked it). It was a rock form of cocaine that was much cheaper than the powder. By the 1990's, opiate pain medications (Vicodin, Percocet, and OxyContin) were being heavily over-prescribed and abused. As regulations began to tighten, addicts began buying them on the streets at grossly inflated prices. This dilemma is what created the heroin epidemic we are battling today.

Drugs that are taken for non-medical purposes are generally used to alter our moods, reduce emotional pain and anxiety, increase socialization, or expand our consciousness to have new experiences. Although anyone can get addicted to drugs, most people don't! For those who do, the pleasurable experience they get from using drugs is far greater than the pain they experience from not using them. Therefore, they are willing to risk health, legal complications, family, jobs, and even their futures in order to continue self-medicating.

Substance addiction can be defined as seeking drug or alcohol consumption compulsively, despite the harmful and dangerous consequences. It is often accompanied by a physical dependence and a need for increasing amounts of that substance to achieve the same effect.

What Are The Drugs We Abuse?

Some of the drugs that are frequently abused have been around a long time. The earliest record of using the Cannabis plant (marijuana) was in Eastern Europe around 700 BC. In the 1930's it began to be imported to the United States by West Indian sailors. By 1965 there were 1 million marijuana smokers in America, and that increased to 26 million by 2009 (according to the U.S. Department of Health and Human Services).

The Center for Disease Control and Prevention reported 23% of High School students smoke marijuana while only 18% smoked cigarettes.

Cocaine is a highly addictive stimulant derived from the coca leaf. People have been chewing coca leaves for thousands of years in Peru and Brazil, where the plant grows naturally. In the mid-nineteenth century an extract was derived that served as an anesthetic, and later at the turn of the century that extract was added to tonics, including soft drinks like Coca-Cola. Cocaine is a very dangerous drug because of the potential side effects such as: cardiac arrest, seizures, infections of the nasal cavities and lungs, hypertension, psychosis, and overdose. In spite of that, in 2007, according to the National Drug Control Policy, there were 36 million people that have used cocaine or its derivative, crack.

There is reference to opium being used to relieve pain as early as 6,000 years ago by the Sumerians. Immigrant Chinese railroad workers introduced smoking opium to Americans in the 1850's and 1860's. Morphine, a chemical extraction from opium, was first marketed in 1827 to treat opium addiction, but not used widely until the invention of the hypodermic needle 30 years later. It was used extensively to treat the wounded in the Civil War, producing approximately 400,000 addicts who suffered with the "soldier's disease".

Heroin was synthesized from morphine in 1874 and marketed 20 years later in America. Initially it was thought to be the answer to morphine addiction, until it was discovered to be twice as strong as morphine and even more highly addictive. By the 1920's many of the New York City addicts supported their habits by collecting scrap metal from industrial junkyards earning the name "junkies" by the authorities. In 1947, methadone was released and thought to be the "cure" for heroin addiction. Though it was soon discovered that at best, methadone could only help to "maintain" an addict, which helped them avoid criminal activity they would otherwise engage in to support their habit.

Narcotic addicts crave opiates because of the intense euphoria and the sense of well-being those drugs deliver to them. It is interesting that our response to opiate addiction has been to create derivative opiates to help those addicted withdraw from that feeling. From opium to morphine to heroin to methadone... that philosophy has never been successful.

In 1893, methamphetamine was first synthesized from ephedrine. During World War II, it was used extensively in the armed forces to treat exhaustion, increase alertness, and elevate moods. It was extremely popular in the 1960's as a dieting drug. Crystal meth is a form of the stimulant used commonly as a party drug, which is highly addictive and has serious side effects, including heart attack, stroke, brain damage, paranoia, psychosis or death. The United Nations considers methamphetamine the most abused hard drug, as there are 26 million meth addicts in the world, which is more than heroin or cocaine addicts combined.

The third most abused substances by teens are inhalants. Huffing involves inhaling volatile substances for their intoxicating effect. The effects can range from alcohol type intoxication to vivid hallucinations, depending on the substance and the dosage. The substances include gases from aerosol cans, gasoline and paint thinners, and glue. These chemicals harm every organ in your body, and the frightening truth is that even a first time use of an inhalant can result in sudden death. Huffing is popular among teens because the substances are legal, easily purchased, and cheap. By the time a student in America reaches the 8th grade, 1 in 5 will have used inhalants. Of those who die from huffing, 22% were first time users.

Prescription drug abuse has risen about 10% every year since 2008, with drugs such as pain killers, tranquilizers, amphetamines, and sedatives growing in popularity. According to a recent study by "Monitoring the Future" prescription drug use is the second most abused category after marijuana. One of the dangers with these drugs is that they are perceived to be safer than street drugs, because they are prescribed by a doctor and they are legal. But 28,000 Americans died from the misuse of prescription drugs in 2009. Often these drugs are mixed with alcohol, the effects of which can be deadly.

> Alcohol is the most commonly abused substance in America, by both adults and teens.

One in every 12 adults (17.6 million people) are alcohol dependent. By 8th grade, 25% of the students have been drunk, and by 12th grade, that number climbs to 62%. Because teens often drink and drive, car accidents are the number one cause of death for 15-20 year olds. Among college students under age 21, there are 50,000 alcohol related date rapes, and 430,000 assaults by students who have been drinking. More than 7 million children are abused or neglected because they live in a home where at least one parent is an alcohol abuser.

Club drugs, or rave drugs, are recreational drugs associated with parties, all night dances and nightclubs. They were first popular in the 1970's at disco clubs but have continued to be used through the 1980's and 1990's at raves. These drugs include ecstasy, ketamine, GHB and rohypnol (the most popular date rape drugs) and "poppers" (nitrites). The National Institute of Drug Abuse reported in 2000 that 6.5 million Americans were using club drugs.

Two drugs that are becoming popular and are being abused are bath salts and krokodil. These drugs are categorized as "designer drugs." These drugs have their chemical compound altered in order to avoid being controlled by laws against illegal drug compounds. Mephedrone (bath salts) is a synthetic form of cathinone, which is an amphetamine. It is sold under a variety of names and can be easily found in a local convenience store. It is highly addictive and dangerous. Krokodil is a homemade version of desomorphine, a derivative of morphine. First synthesized in America in 1932, it is much cheaper and more potent than heroin. There is a current epidemic in Russia where it can easily be made from over the counter codeine. It causes your skin to have a green and scaly look, like a crocodile's. With continued use the skin can begin to rot. Amputations are common among those who are addicted to krokodil.

The Bureau of Justice Statistics has published a report "Drug Use: Youth" (High school seniors used within the past year)

Alcohol – 70%

Marijuana – 35%

Stimulants/Opiates – 10%

Tranquilizers/Sedatives – 10%

Hallucinogens – 6%

Cocaine – 5%

Inhalants – 4%

Steroids – 3%

Heroin – 1%

These statistics show that we need to recognize that 90% of Americans with a substance abuse problem started smoking, drinking, or using drugs before the age of 18.

Globally, the United States has the highest levels of illegal drug use, three times greater than Europe's. In 2012, there were 23.9 million Americans aged 12 and over who were using illegal drugs, and 10 million who were alcoholic. Clearly, the war on drugs that began 40 years ago in the Nixon administration has not yet been won.

What Are The Costs and Effects of Addiction?

It would be nice to think the costs of addiction are confined to the addicts themselves. However, nothing would be further from the truth. Every family and community in America is affected either directly or indirectly. Substance abuse is an equal opportunity destroyer, no population group is immune to its damage. Addiction contributes to many of the current and ongoing challenges our nation faces today. The New York Times published a data report from the Federal and State Financing on Substance Abuse and Addiction in May, 2009, which declared the following losses: (In billions of dollars)

$207.2 – Health Care (medical treatment, drug rehabilitation programs, insurance). For example, pill addicts who shop around for doctors to obtain prescriptions costs insurers $10,000 – $15,000 each annually. This increases health care premiums for us all.

$47.0 – Justice Department (courts, public safety, and penal system) The average cost to house an inmate in New England is $47,000. Sixty percent of the inmates in federal prisons are there for drug related crimes. These crimes are not only for sales or possession of illegal drugs, but for robbery, theft, home invasions, prostitution, assault and homicide.

$46.7 – Children and Family Assistance – Child

Protective Services documents 50-80% of all cases of child abuse and neglect involved parents who were alcohol and drug abusers. In cases of domestic violence 55-85% are alcohol or drug related. Babies who are born to mothers who are substance abusers have high premature birth rates, low birth weight, and various other health problems.

$33.9 – Education and Prevention – In 2011 President Obama allocated $15.5 billion toward the "War on Drugs," of which $5.5 billion would be geared toward prevention and treatment. None of the government's prevention programs to date have shown any documented evidence of ongoing success (including "Just Say No" and "D.A.R.E." (Drug Abuse Resistance Education), and have cost the taxpayers billions of dollars.

$22.6 – Other - The study did not indicate what these other costs are.

$5.1 – Regulating alcohol and tobacco products and collecting those taxes.

$2.6 – Drug trafficking prevention – The United Nations Office on Drugs and Crime targets importation of illegal drugs into America. With an average budget in this one department of $160 million their strategy remains the same; to target Afghanistan and Myanmar for 90% of the opium (heroin), Colombia and Peru for the coca leaf growth (cocaine), and Poland and other Eastern European countries for amphetamine production. Their interest is in shutting down the global suppliers, which is the third aspect of their plan. The first is prevention aimed at our youth, and second is treatment for those who are already addicted. They have 166 countries working cooperatively but their success has been modest at best.

In a 2008 brief by the National Institute of Drug Abuse encouraging Employee Assistant Programs, they estimated an annual loss of $197 billion from employees who were substance abusers due to absenteeism, poor job performance, work related injuries, double health care costs, and frequent job turnovers.

There are 40 million people annually whose illnesses, accidents, and deaths are related to tobacco, drugs, and alcohol.

Heroin overdoses have caused an overwhelming number of deaths in the last few years.

Finally, how do we assign a dollar amount to the children and families that are destroyed because of the dysfunctional and damaging behaviors of the family members who are addicts? What about the lost quality of life? Clearly the cost and effect of addiction reaches far beyond the addict and into the lives of their family and friends, their local communities, and our nation.

Our Current Epidemic

Our current challenge with addiction is a frightening one… particularly in the New England area where we are in the clutches of a heroin epidemic. In Maine, heroin overdoses quadrupled between 2011 and 2012. A few years ago in New Hampshire overdose deaths from heroin were in the single digits. In 2012 they had 37 deaths and last year (2013) 63 people died from heroin. In January 2014, Vermont Governor Pete Shumlin dedicated his State of the Union address to the "full blown heroin crisis." Heroin overdoses have doubled there from 2012 to 2013. Accidental drug overdoses increased 38% in Connecticut from 2012 through 2013, with 257 deaths last year. Connecticut's U.S. Senators are calling for more federal money and other assistance to battle a growing heroin epidemic in their state and across the nation.

For the first three months of 2014 Rhode Island lost 72 people to opiate overdoses, more than twice the usual number. Rhode Island State Police Colonel Steven O'Donnell said, "The number of overdose deaths was ten times the homicide rate in the state." Heroin claimed 190 lives in Massachusetts from November 2013 through February 2014. Boston's mayor launched a campaign for the entire city to fight against opiate overdoses, stating that he wanted NARCAN (naloxone, a drug that can reverse heroin overdoses) kits inside police cruisers, fire trucks, and the homes of addicts. Although NARCAN does save lives, it doesn't address the problem of addiction. That problem is deeply rooted in the addicts themselves, and it can't be cured by another drug. United States Senator Edward J. Markey stated, "Heroin is a curse upon America unlike anything that had been seen before."

So why the drastic increase in heroin addiction? We mentioned previously that in the 1990's addictive painkillers were loosely prescribed generating millions of pill addicts, otherwise known as "Generation RX." As regulations began to tighten on physicians, the demand became greater than the legitimate supply, driving those addicted to the streets to find relief. The price for the narcotic pills sold illegitimately on the streets was extremely high compared to the cost of a legitimate prescription (One OxyContin tablet could cost you $30).

At that point, heroin becomes an easy and reasonable answer because it is plentiful, easily available, and most importantly, cheap (you can buy a stamp-sized bag for $5). The problem is that when the addict was taking opiate pills they knew what they were taking as each dosage in the pill was the same. When taking heroin, you never know what you are getting. It depends on how pure the product was to begin with, what it was cut with, and how much it was cut.

The danger lies in the fact that a bag from one dealer could be equivalent in opiate content to three bags bought from another dealer. Currently, the deadly additive to heroin causing so many of the recent deaths, is Fentanyl. Fentanyl is used primarily for pre and post-surgical procedures. For example, in New England heroin purity is about 15% but in New Jersey it is anywhere from 40-50%. New Jersey views heroin and opiate abuse as "the number one health care crisis" in its state, where it has increased 700% in the last decade. From 2010 through 2013 New Jersey saw 4,300 drug related deaths. These addicts are no longer the stereotypical urban minorities from lower income families, but rather white, young, educated suburbanites. The fact that some recent celebrities have died from heroin overdoses has brought attention to that fact, most notably, "Glee" TV star, Cory Monteith. According to an analysis published in the journal JAMA Psychiatry, during the last decade 90% of new heroin users were white, and heroin overdoses have climbed by 45% between 2006 and 2010.

In regard to addiction, we are in an unprecedented epidemic. "Drugs destroy lives and communities, undermine sustainable human development and generate crime. Drugs affect all sectors of society in all countries, in particular, drug abuse affects the freedom and development of our young people, the world's most valuable asset..." (Opening to Political Declaration adopted by United Nations General Assembly, June 10, 1998).

We will continue to be flooded by drugs of all kinds as long as there is a demand for them. Until we target the heart of the matter that causes people to use drugs in the first place, we can never hope to win a battle much, less the war. Social problems such as childhood sexual and physical abuse, broken and fatherless homes, poverty, victimization of all kinds, are all factors and are rooted in sin.

That is why Teen Challenge has always believed that a personal relationship with Jesus Christ is the only long-term answer and why we claim to have a "cure for addiction." It is not our program that sets people free from their addictions, but rather the Person they meet when they come to the program… Jesus. It is not our staff that changes addicts when they come through our doors, but rather the power of God's Holy Spirit who encounters them and transforms their hearts.

The government does not have an answer for this crisis, but God does. Teen Challenge can offer hope to every addict because of what God has said in His word, "May the God of hope fill you with all joy and peace as you trust in Him, so that you may overflow with hope by the power of the Holy Spirit." Romans 15:13

Chapter 1
In the Beginning

Sandy Segrest

"This whole, strange adventure got its start late one night when I was sitting in my study reading a Life magazine, and turned a page. At first glance, it seemed that there was nothing on the page to interest me. It carried a pen drawing of a trial-taking place in New York City, 350 miles away."

This brief opening paragraph, and the other quotes to follow, is from David Wilkerson's *The Cross and the Switchblade.*

David Wilkerson introduces his true and compelling story of the beginning of Teen Challenge in 1958. The "adventure" mentioned in the first sentence continues today around the world and has impacted tens of thousands of lives.

Rev. Wilkerson describes in his book the attempts made to speak with seven teenaged gang members on trial for murdering a handicapped boy named Michael Farmer. Wilkerson, a Pennsylvania country preacher, was continually thwarted in his multiple efforts to see those young teenagers. Yet he discovered he had gained infamy when his publicized first attempt to see them resulted in his being thrown unceremoniously from the trial's courtroom. That notoriety gained this preacher first, credibility and then, an audience with other gang members and drug addicts he encountered on the streets of New York City.

"Their [the teenagers] logic was simple: The cops didn't like me; the cops didn't like them. We were in the same boat."

The dramatic conversion and transformation of Nicky Cruz, a notorious gang leader in Brooklyn, was a primary example in *The Cross and the Switchblade*, of the impact Wilkerson had on troubled lives who had once been thought of as hopeless.

David Wilkerson moved to New York to work fulltime among gang members sharing a message of God's love for them. Over the next few years, the growing epidemic of drug addiction began to decimate the gangs in New York, forcing addicts into a solitary existence where they struggled to satisfy the demand for drugs their minds and bodies craved. The fledgling Teen Challenge organization and Wilkerson adapted to this new reality seeking to make their efforts effective for those bound by drug addiction.

First, a former mansion was purchased in Brooklyn which became a refuge for addicts seeking to change their lives. Then, a working farm in Pennsylvania was established in 1962. Those who overfilled the Brooklyn home and were growing in their new faith were transferred to this rural location. A more structured program was developed and coordinated by the two locations to help their young residents overcome addictions and to learn to successfully live as drug-free Christians in the real world. As the program took further shape, it became a one-year residential recovery effort.

"Certainly we cannot claim a magical cure for addiction. The devil, which hides in the needle, the pills and the powder, is so deadly strong that any such claim would be foolish. All we can say is that we have found a power that captures a person more strongly than narcotics but He captures only to liberate."

Continuing today, a favorite passage at all Teen Challenge locations is

"Therefore, if anyone is in Christ, he is a new creation: the old has gone, the new has come! All this is from God, who reconciled us to himself through Christ and gave us the ministry of reconciliation."
2 Corinthians 5:17,18

The Message of God's Love and Hope
Travels Far from Brooklyn

The popularity of *The Cross and the Switchblade* was a phenomenon fueled to a great extent by word of mouth.

• *The Cross and the Switchblade* was published in 1962. Today more than 16 million have been sold and distributed in over thirty languages.

• In 1970 a film adaptation was released with Pat Boone as David Wilkerson and Erik Estrada as Nicky Cruz. An estimated 50 million people in more than 150 countries have seen it.

• In 1972 the book was adapted into a comic book.

• In 1968 Nicky Cruz published his own popular autobiography, *Run Baby Run*.

The story of what God was doing through the Teen Challenge ministry in New York captured hearts and excited a passion to see the same ministry established in other locations. Thousands of people from around the nation, and then eventually around the world, flocked to Brooklyn to see for themselves what was happening. Teen Challenge Centers were quickly established in Chicago, Los Angeles and Boston, all offering hope to both the addicted and their despairing families.

In 1969, Howard and Pat Foltz, leaders of the Teen Challenge ministry in Dallas moved to Holland to open a Teen

Challenge coffeehouse, an outreach ministry. Eventually they moved to Germany and founded Continental Teen Challenge to foster the growing Teen Challenge ministry in Europe.

In 1973, a national coordinating office was established in Missouri. This office provides a curriculum for Teen Challenge sites and establishes criteria for program standards. There are more than 200 locations in the United States today. A listing of those locations can be found at http://teenchallengeusa.com/locations.

In 1995 Don Wilkerson, brother to David Wilkerson, and a long-time respected leader of the ministry in the United States established Global Teen Challenge. Its US office is now in the state of Georgia and provides many services to Teen Challenges in the US, as well as around the world.

The ministry has grown exponentially with more than 1,000 Teen Challenge sites in 104 countries around the world. A listing of those locations can be found at: http://globaltc.org/html/global_locations.htm

The same message of God's love, mercy and power, which was first preached in 1958, still transforms lives and still yields the same miracles over and over.

This message has found receptive hearts in every culture and language where it has been shared.

Teen Challenge throughout
New England and New Jersey

The fourth Teen Challenge established in the United States was ideally situated in Boston to reach that large metropolitan area and its great need. From that cornerstone ministry in Boston, help and services began to be extended throughout New England.

David Milley, assisted by brothers Ernie, Steve and Joe Tavilla were God-driven and worked tirelessly to see that Teen Challenge was established throughout New England. From that beginning, a message of the Lord's power to transform lives began to invade each state and community. Under the leadership of Dr. Rodney Hart new sites in Brockton, Massachusetts, Rhode Island, Connecticut and New Hampshire were added by 2002. Then, in 2004 a unique opportunity arose and a Teen Challenge was planted at the Dartmouth House of Corrections. Then from 2004-2007 the ministry further expanded to including new locations in Vermont, Maine and New Jersey.

Together these residential homes provide both a refuge and the opportunity for 400 drug and alcohol addicted adults to begin life all over again. However, now they will be equipped with God's forgiveness and His power to help them overcome their life controlling problems.

Dynamic outreaches are conducted in every state,

providing drug education and prevention efforts to youth and at-risk teens in troubled neighborhoods. Additionally, support services are provided for the families of drug or alcohol addicted individuals in many sites.

These efforts are supported by thousands of caring individuals, churches and businesses that see the value and potential in each life. Teen Challenge New England and New Jersey depends on contributions – small and large – to enable our arms and doors to stay wide open to receive hurting individuals who desperately need to know there is hope.

Hope

In this day when drug addiction and abuse has crossed every geographic, economic, cultural and ethnic barrier, Teen Challenge is a refuge where freedom can be found. God can, and does, do miracles.

There is hope for those who have grown up in drug-infested communities or in families where substance abuse is common, change can happen. Life and situations don't have to remain the same.

There is hope for those who come from loving homes and good communities but have become trapped in the spiral of addiction. What may have begun as an act of rebellion or harmless experimentation has now become a bondage that is robbing them of their futures and ripping them from their families. It is possible to get back on the right track.

There is hope that every person who struggles with addiction, regardless of ethnicity, social status or age, can be free because they have a Father, God, Who cares deeply about His children.

The Real Story of Teen Challenge

The real story of Teen Challenge is a story about God and His power to change lives. This story is exemplified many times each day in the lives that have been transformed at Teen Challenge locations throughout New England, New Jersey, and around the world.

We pray the stories in this book of "Changed Lives" show off God in a way that gives you hope for your own impossible situations, as well as refresh the faith in your heart. Then your story can also be a one of God's love and His ever-present help in times of trouble.

Chapter 2
Dead End Street

Rich Welch

The innocence of childhood and a happy family were the greatest joys of my early years. Little did I know at that time, that unpredictable events would affect my destiny. I experienced what it means to live a checkered life, good and evil, up and down, rich and poor, and bound and free – as some would say, yin and yang. It seemed like an eternity of trips around the same-old-block with my afflictions and addictions. Finally, I emerged on the other side with a "Changed Life;" rescued, restored and given a second chance. My arrival at Teen Challenge was the day my life would change forever. I am living proof of what the power of God, prayer and a personal relationship with Jesus Christ can do. The good news is, there is HOPE and help for anyone who may be following the same path I once traveled.

The Early Years

We are driving past the Coast Guard Academy in New London, Connecticut. The sight of the Coast Guard uniformed cadets marching across the beautiful sprawling green lawn with the great brick structure that housed the classrooms in the background was the breathtaking picture I saw. This, I hoped, would be my future. I was about 9 years old, the year was 1965. At that time, more than anything thing else, I wanted to become a Coast Guard Cadet. Just a week before, I was sitting in the stands at a Coast Guard Bears football game with my dad and my two brothers, when an older man in uniform came and shook hands with my father. After a few words, he turned his attention our way. That man was Otto Graham, NFL Hall of Fame quarterback and then head coach for the team. "How are you boys doing? Do you like football?" Not realizing at the time who he was, I spoke up and said, "I love football and someday I'll be playing on this field." Otto replied, "Well if you study real hard, and practice, your dream can come true."

That was many years ago, and so much has happened since that time. That dream never did come true, but what the Lord has done in my life is nothing short of a miracle. Today I'm living a new dream.

I was born in New London, Connecticut, in 1956. My father was an electrician, my mother a stay-at-home mom, who took care of my two brothers, my sister, and me. We lived in a small three-bedroom house on a side street in a middle-class neighborhood. "The Brothers", as we called ourselves, always shared a bedroom that was a good venue for horsing around, fighting, laughing and sneaking things into the room that we weren't allowed to have. We were all very close in age, just a year apart, but we got along well in our early years.

We grew up playing sports. My dad, Richard, better known as Jack, was an athlete and so we followed suit. We were always active in the major sports: basketball, football, and baseball. I remember my dad spending endless hours on the court or field with us, practicing and playing in minor league, little league, and peewee football.

I was raised Roman Catholic and went to Catholic elementary and high schools. I was an altar boy and served at Mass and also at weddings and funerals, which resulted in "tips" for our services.

I was a good student who never really had to study too hard to get good grades. This kept my parents off my back and everyone happy. I was also a hard worker. I would mow lawns, shovel snow, and had two paper routes to make extra money. I was never afraid of hard work and the extra cash was welcome. So, between home-life, school and sports, life was hectic but happy.

Doom Descends

Then one afternoon, my whole life changed forever. I was walking home from practice and a friend of the family picked me up – we called him "uncle." He took me out to a secluded place not far from my home and sexually assaulted me. My whole world turned upside down. I didn't know what to do. I cried and I was so frightened that I felt like my head was going to bust open. He told me if I ever said anything, he would hurt my younger brothers, my dad would lose his job, and we would all end up in the "poor house." I was mortified.

> That day, I lost my innocence, and began
> a journey of pain and suffering that no child
> should ever have to endure.

I was in such a state of confusion and shock, I didn't know what to do. I walked back to the baseball field where I had come from and sat in the dugout for what seemed to be hours, trying to figure out what to do next. That night at home in bed, as the incident played over and over in my mind, the voice I would come to hate more than anything in my life, echoed his threatening words. I would be in bondage to that awful man for the next three years of my life. Every time it happened, I became more and more angry. I could tell no one.

I had no place to vent. I was truly in agony.

Time Marches On

In the 7th grade, I began abusing substances. A couple of the older guys were out back of the school smoking cigarettes when I walked around the corner and surprised them. These were two of the really "cool guys" who never paid me much attention. They were really concerned I would tell on them, but after a bit of threatening on their part, they offered me a smoke instead. So, despite being new to smoking, rather than blow this opportunity to do as the cool guys did, I said "yes" and had my first smoke, a Marlboro. I remember coughing and getting so dizzy that I felt like passing out, but I hung on and kept it together. After that day I went to another level in the eyes of the cool guys – and my life started to change.

I started drinking beer, smoking weed, taking Quaaludes and popping some speed on the side. I remember coming home "wrecked" after a party and my brothers just staring at me, not knowing what to say. Then, I stole a bottle of wine from the back of the sanctuary where the priests and the altar boys would prepare to serve Mass. Along with the wine, I took a bag of the larger hosts – the bread element – and went to a back corner of the church building hidden from sight. I proceeded to have communion, consuming wine and host alike, only to be awakened by the Monsignor standing over me. This only served to boost my reputation, which led me into more trouble.

While under the influence, I now had the courage to stand up to my "uncle", the man that brutalized and abused me, and say "No more!" I was not going to take it anymore, and I threatened him. High on a pocketful of "crossroads" (speed), when he stopped by the basketball court, I threatened him, yelled, and beat on the hood of that disgusting pickup truck that had been a chamber of horrors for so long. My hunger for revenge would eventually lead me to sink his boat and beat him up outside of a local bar he frequented. Finally, it was over.

As I moved into adolescence, the need to prove my manhood rose quickly. All of a sudden, girls became a top priority in my life. I found myself slipping away from all those things that had been important to me in the past. I was a freshman at St. Bernard High School and the amount of drugs and alcohol available to me tripled. Many of the students there came from wealthy families and the quality and quantity of the available drugs was better. At that time, hallucinogens were the thing to do. This was post Woodstock, where "free love" and an "anything goes" attitude was a way of life.

When I turned 14 years old, I abandoned sports, gravitated towards rock music, and grew long hair. Being so damaged from the abuse, feeling so dirty and guilty, I set out to quickly prove that I was more manly and stronger than any-one else. At 15 years old, I met a redheaded Irish girl who had her own problems at home and was unhappy. I remember even at that early age starting to talk about marriage. Around that time, I found myself in trouble and suspended from my all boys high school because I brought her to an open house there and got into a fight with the principal, after he tried to choke me. At 16 years old, I stopped going to school alto-gether and got a job at the Neutron Manufacturing Company. At 17 years old, I married the lassie wearing a yellow tuxedo and a ruffled seventies-style shirt.

I did return to school, trying to better myself, and ac-quired my high school diploma. When I turned 18 years old, I started an apprenticeship as a plumber/pipefitter. This was made easier because my grandfather, Albert Benvenutti, es-sentially started the United Association of Plumbers and Pip-efitters Local 302 in his own living room in 1924.

My wife became pregnant and wasn't working, so I took another job at night pumping gas. I remember those long hard days; working myself into a state of exhaustion to provide for my wife and soon-to-be-born baby. As the months went by, I watched my peers go to their proms, excel at sports, and go on to college. It drove me further along down the path of my addictions, attempting to alleviate some of my pain and regrets.

My son, Richard Thomas Welch, was born on October 31, 1975, at Laurence Memorial Hospital in New London, Connecticut. I couldn't believe I was now a father. I remember looking at that beautiful, tiny baby boy and wondering how was I ever going to be a father to him. Our marriage was headed south due to many issues, including my brother, money, alcohol and drugs. We soon broke up. My brother and my wife got together and eventually they married. This was another catalyst in my life that led to my death-wish-like determination to escape my problems and inflict pain and harm on myself for many years to come.

Dark Territory

Embarrassed and humiliated by all that had transpired in my marriage, I moved away to West Virginia to work on the construction of a new nuclear power plant and then on to Chicago. We were union workers called U.A. Boomers, traveling the country looking to work on the big nuclear powerhouse projects where the overtime was plentiful and the money was big. This work funded my cocaine and eventually my heroin habits launching me into a terrifying world of addiction that I had never known before and wouldn't wish on anyone.

In 1981, I got into rock 'n' roll and joined an indie rock band, The Cartoons; I was the drummer. We played all original material, and recorded an ELP (extended play record).We did really well on college radio, the college circuit, and mini regional tours. We played some big venues: CBGBs, The Ritz and The Living Room, in New York City; The Paradise and The Channel, in Boston; Toad's Place, in New Haven; and the beaches in Rhode Island. My drug use ran rampant and my life was a dual existence between a career in mechanical contracting and music. Drugs were the source of endurance and escape; I was using them to function and functioning to use them. After about six years, the band disbursed and all the hopes and dreams that were associated with it died.

I had several relationships with women that went badly, and already having a failed marriage, I vowed never to make that mistake again. My son was growing up and I made many attempts to see him, obtain visitation rights and tried to be a dad. Sometimes it would be all right, other times it was horrible.

> The guilt and shame that I experienced was
> so great at times it felt as if I were going insane
> or would just simply burst, and die.

In 1988 I entered my first detoxification and drug rehab program at Edgehill in Newport. This was one of the most exclusive rehab programs in the eastern part of the United States and it came with a price tag around $28,000 for 30 days. Yet, within the first three hours of finishing Edgehill, I found myself in a hotel room shooting heroin again. Over the next 10 years I entered over 70 more detoxes and programs, everything from exclusive rehabs to state run mental institutions. They put me on all kinds of medication for depression, anxiety, schizophrenia, bi-polar; you name it, they prescribed it. Psychotherapy, group therapy, psychiatry, Christian Science, self-help books, positive thinking, Narcotics Anonymous, Alcohol Anonymous, and Cocaine Anonymous. At the meetings they would say, "welcome back" and "keep coming back." I was coming and going so much my head spun. Nothing was working. I just kept getting high, and kept running. I was so tired and wondered, how long could I go on? What would bring my tragic story to an end?

I had a lot of hate and bitterness inside. I was angry. At times, I was able to hide my feelings, but mostly, I would use drugs to numb the pain. Over and over I kept trying to establish a relationship with my son, Ricky, but I only kept hurting him time and time again. Never in my life would I have thought that I would end up a drug addict. After having so many aspirations to do great things with my life, I hated what I had become. Helpless and hopeless, with no purpose, I was trapped with no way out and there was no end in sight... I just wanted to die.

I was so sick of hurting the people in my life who managed to continue to love and care about me: my mother, my father, my sister, Shirley, who could never give up on me, and my nephew and niece, Doug and Michelle. At this point, I was working and living on and off with my parents. I was using more than ever and started habitually stealing from my parents. Then one day when I came home, my mother had locked the door. She said: "We love you, but we just can't do this anymore. We cannot watch you kill yourself. You are not welcome in our home." I was devastated. I said, "How can you do this to me?" I saw the tears run down her face and it absolutely broke my heart. With all my pent up anger, I now hated myself more than ever.

I had once said, "I will never put a needle in my body to get high…" but I did. "I will never end up in jail…" but I did. "I will never be homeless and sleep in a shelter…" but I did. This went on for about eight months: couch surfing, house hopping, and sleeping in Salvation Army boxes or anything else I could find. As I walked down the lonely cold streets at night alone, sick, hopeless and wanting to die, with every step I took, my situation and self-hate grew. My life became so gut-wrenching I would actually get physically sick to my stomach. I weighed 128 pounds, I had overdosed twice and I was going to die.

I remember my mother, in her seventies, handing me sandwiches out of her window with tears running down her face, asking "How I had come to this?" It reminded me how

45

destitute my life was. I remembered from my time as a Catholic altar boy how to pray, so I did! "If you are real God, help me!"

Back from the Brink

My son Ricky was going to the University of Rhode Island. He had a roommate who was a born-again Christian and he led my son to the Lord. He began attending an Assembly of God church near the school. Like me, he was musical, and when he saw the church band and heard the worship music at the church, he became excited. He never knew that this kind of music was played in churches. One Sunday morning while he was at the church, a ministry called Teen Challenge had come in with a group of about 12 men. They sang in a choir and told their stories of how God had delivered them from addiction.

Over the years, Ricky had learned about my addiction and the many attempts I had made to get clean and sober, to get my life together. After listening to the men he said to himself, "That could be my dad up there, saying what these men were saying.

'My dad needs God in his life; it is the only thing that is ever going to help him.' "

He was so excited he drove to my hometown of New London to see if he could find me. By this time I was a complete wreck, bankrupt in every area of my life, homeless and hopeless, with no future in sight. I was walking down the street and I heard his noisy car and saw him driving, but I didn't want him to see me because I was in such bad shape. I quickly attempted to get away, turning down a street and there, staring me in the face, was a big yellow sign that read "Dead End." It was symbolic for my entire life, there was nowhere to run or hide any longer. I was truly at a dead end.

My son stopped the car, ran up to me, and threw his arms around me saying, "Dad, I love you, and I found a place for you to go. You need God, Dad." "God?" I said, "There is no God. How could God let me get like this?" He told me that he forgave me and that all he wanted was for me to get my life right. I broke down and started to cry, then he started crying. I told him how sorry I was for all the pain, for all the times that I left him waiting for me, and for all the times I disappointed him and hurt him.

Then I felt something really strange. It felt as though someone had taken an electric blanket and wrapped it around me. For the first time since I was nine years old, I felt warm and safe. Then I heard a beautiful voice that said, "It's going to be all right, it's going to be all right." I didn't know it then, but I now know, that was God's voice talking to me.

My son told me to get in the car and before I knew it, I was on the phone with Teen Challenge. They told me to call everyday while I was waiting for a bed to become available. Each day I called, a woman named Edith answered the phone. I remember she was always so kind and gentle. She would encourage me to keep calling and not to give up, and she would always sneak in a little prayer and something about God that I didn't really understand at the time. I don't know what it was, but I always seemed to feel better after I talked to Edith and actually looked forward to the call the next day. Her warmth was so welcomed and seemed to bring a light in the midst of my cold darkness.

Then finally a call came from Teen Challenge and an intake coordinator told me there was room and to come in.

I remember I called my sister and then went to see my mother. I will never forget what she said to me on the front porch that day. She said, "Rick, your life is a mess and your story is a tragedy, turn the page and begin a new chapter." That's exactly what happened, but from now on, God would be the author.

Into The Light

My sister, Shirley, had agreed to drive me to Teen Challenge. She never gave up on me and I am so grateful to God for her. She had brought me to many of the programs that I attended in the past. She would always stop and buy me a carton of cigarettes before each treatment and this day was no different. I did not recall anyone telling me that smoking was not allowed in Teen Challenge, they probably did, but I just didn't remember. So I walked in the admissions office with the big red box under my arm and a man approached me and said, "Welcome to Teen Challenge, what is that under your arm?"

"Those are my cigarettes," I replied.

"Well you can't smoke here at the program, brother."

I quickly responded, "First of all, I'll smoke anywhere I please, and second of all, I'm not your brother. If I can't smoke here, then I am not staying here." When I turned around to leave, my sister was standing square behind me and she said, "Are you going to let those cigarettes stand in the way of you getting your life together?" After a beat, I gave my sister the cigarettes. I laid them down. Little did I know, those cigarettes would be the first of many things I would lay down.

Teen Challenge was like no other program I'd been in. I saw things in my first few days that I had never seen at any of the programs that I had been to before. People were singing, praying, studying, working, and going to church; everyone appeared to have purpose there. The students seemed happy and able to embrace the structure of the program, and there was a lot of structure. I had never experienced people, especially drug addicts, in such a happy state without being under the influence. I was convinced there must have been alcohol and drugs hidden somewhere there. But after more investigation, I concluded that there were no drugs or alcohol influencing anyone there – the only influence was that of the Holy Spirit.

I began to listen to the leaders as they explained that I needed to be born again. I asked the Lord into my heart and life that September of 1998. I began to read the Word of God and develop a relationship with Jesus Christ. I worked through those tough issues in my life that I never really could talk about with anyone else before. I felt so loved and cared for. I realized that there was a plan for my life, a good and perfect plan. Jeremiah 29:11 became one of my life verses: "For I know the plans I have for you," declares the Lord, "plans to prosper you and not to harm you, plans to give you hope and a future." I came to believe those words. As I grew in the program and as I grew in the Word, I came to a place where I trusted God as His plan was worked out in my life.

Before I knew it, I had my family back in my life; they would visit and phone me. I began to feel much healthier. I gained weight and I had energy and ambition. I was alive again. I had hope for the first time in my adult life. My pride decreased and I became transformed. I started to love and care about the people in Teen Challenge. I learned through

God's Word how to forgive the people who hurt me and that I held responsible for the troubles in my life. I learned not only how to forgive but to also take responsibility for my own actions and the choices I had made.

> I later became the director of the very same choir that my son had seen that Sunday in Rhode Island.

Through the ministry at Teen Challenge I had finally found my purpose. I began to gain the trust of others, which made a huge difference in my attitude and my sense of significance. The Lord was bringing me back to life and restoring me in so many ways. I developed relationships in Teen Challenge that will last a lifetime. There are special people in my life today that I can call and talk to anytime that I am in need.

Graduation from Teen Challenge was an extremely important event in my life. I graduated at our annual banquet at the Villa Bianca Restaurant in front of several hundred people, including my mother, father, sister, brother and other family members. In my former life I was a great starter but a lousy finisher, but here I was actually finishing something that I started. God, working through Teen Challenge, helped me learn how to break that pattern in my life. I am not perfect today, but at least now I finish most of what I start. After graduation, I began a Teen Challenge internship and decided it was where I wanted to work the rest of my life. It helped form my leadership abilities and taught me so much about loving and caring for people. I started as a maintenance supervisor and eventually became a program supervisor. God taught me so much as I grew nearer and nearer to Him. As James 4:8 says, "Come near to God and He will come near to you."

Redemption and Renewal

For many years it was my desire to become a husband and a father. I had never been in a healthy relationship with a woman and didn't even know what it was like. I felt that the Lord would have to be enough for me and having Jesus in my heart was sufficient. When I truly came to that place, God brought my wife, Carrie, into my life. I met her at a tent meeting while on ministry in Vermont. I was leading the Teen Challenge choir and she was there with the praise and worship team from her church. We talked for a while and I really enjoyed our conversation. The next day we were scheduled to do a service at a town hall in the neighboring community and much to my delight, she was there as well. We ran into each other at several other places during the choir's two-week visit to Vermont. Was this coincidence? I recall having a conversation and praying with her the evening we were returning to Connecticut. During our prayer, I opened my eyes to peek at her and when I saw her angelic face praying with such sincerity, I knew in my heart that this was not a coincidence but a divine appointment. We entered into a long distance courtship and when I transitioned to Vermont, we were married.

What a great day it was when our son, Timothy, was born the following year. God is so faithful. My heart's desire was fulfilled at last. I remember on the day of his birth, looking at him and Carrie and thinking about the miracles God had done in my life. The two of them are certainly evidence of God's faithfulness.

Soon after, I became the executive director of a brand new Teen Challenge in Vermont, which opened its doors on January 3, 2005. We have 10.5 acres of beautiful land on the "Holy Hill" in Johnson, Vermont. During the first five years, there was tremendous growth as the Lord's hand guided us. There came a point where we needed to expand and we purchased an additional building. I have been so blessed to see the vision of this ministry come alive and to help so many people come out of the bondage of addiction and into freedom in one of the most afflicted states in the country.

From that dead end street, to where the Lord has me today is nothing short of a miracle. The only explanation for my life is a supernatural one. He has brought me from the mental institute to the minister's institute. Mine is a life that has been "Changed" from a helpless, homeless drug addict, to a godly husband, father and grandfather, an ordained Assembly of God minister, an executive director overseeing two Teen Challenge campuses and most importantly a servant of the Most High God. I'm living a dream.

Today I have the immense privilege of serving the students, the hard working staff members of this awesome ministry and to serve alongside leaders who are men and women of God. If I boast today I boast in the Lord.

I pray that my story would bring hope to those who see no way out, those who are lost and bound up in addictions. Through the love of the Lord Jesus Christ and the transforming power of His Word, may you come to the place of freedom and living a dream - from dead end to no end.

"Now to him who is able to do immeasurably more than all we ask or imagine, according to his power that is at work in us... " Ephesians 3:20

Thank You Lord Jesus, Carrie, Ricky, Timothy and my Teen Challenge family.

Chapter 3
Broken

Tabatha Mello

My first memories consist of fear, abandonment, hunger and a longing for love. They take me back to an apartment in the projects of Worcester, Massachusetts, where I lived. Drug addicts were constantly in and out of my house, buying drugs and shooting up heroin on my couch. There were times I was so hungry and all I could find in the house was a handful of oatmeal. Sometimes a bottle of mustard was the only thing to eat, and I would squeeze it into my mouth to try to satisfy the hunger pains. There were never peaceful nights of sleep, since the police were banging on my front door and strange men were walking in and out of my bedroom.

Eventually the police caught up with my mother, who was constantly in and out of jail, and I was put into the foster care system. I wish I could say there was some safety and refuge in my foster home but instead it filled me with even more fear. I was horribly neglected. I was made to sleep in the basement in a soiled, urine stained bed, with my other foster brothers and sisters. The basement was dingy, and once again, I remember feeling hungry. I have vivid memories of being about five years old and suffering abuse in that house. I was made to wait hand and foot on the foster parents and do things like massage their feet. Sometimes, they would lock me outside by myself, while everyone else would eat. The abuse came to a head, when one day the foster family punished me by holding my head underwater in their pool. When they finally let me come up for breath, I was hyperventilating. I thought for sure I was going to die that day.

After that incident, my caseworker moved me to another foster home and placed me with the LaMier Family. This home was completely opposite of anything I had experienced in life thus far. I was welcomed with warm hugs, gifts and so much love. Yet I was so broken inside. I was already so cold and hardened that I didn't know how to receive any of the affection. I didn't know how to feel safe and I only wished I could have my mother back. At that time, it was explained to me that she was in jail and might be back for me once she got out. Two years later, at the age of seven, I was officially adopted. If my mother ever came looking for me, I would not be able to go back to her. This devastated me and I felt so alone. I wrote to Santa Claus asking for my mother back instead of gifts. I did the same thing with every fictional character that was introduced to me and brought me goodies, I always asked if I could have my mother back instead.

With the feeling of deep rejection setting in, I wasn't able to grow close to my adoptive parents. They asked me to call them Mom and Dad but I couldn't; it was too difficult for me. Growing up they were very strict and didn't allow me to do a lot outside of my home. I had a few friends in the neighborhood, but for the most part, was warned to stay inside because of my background of addiction. they were concerned for my well-being. I became very rebellious in school and hung out with other kids who were troubled like myself. I remember trying my first drink at around 12 years old. Instead of going home after school, went to a friend's house and we drank. I don't remember much about that day. What I do know is I blacked out, and I woke up in my bed with leaves and vomit on me and in my hair. I had no pants on and I knew that I had been raped.

> That was the first day I actually felt guilt and shame, it cut so deep, and I just buried it.

My family didn't speak about the incident, and I went back to school as if nothing ever happened. Soon I began looking for a reason to leave home. When I asked my father if

Changed Lives

I could go to a football game, he said no. That was the night I decided I would leave. I wanted to escape all of my guilt and look for something to fill the void in my life. I jumped out of my bedroom window and never looked back.

Since that day I left home, I found everything but peace; only substances filled that void in my life. I rotated living in and out of juvenile detention centers and different foster homes. I committed small crimes, slept around, and hung out with gang members, while bouncing all over the state. My parents were devastated that I had left, but I was completely indifferent to their feelings and felt no remorse for my actions. I tried many different drugs, from coke to LSD, and went "all-in" every time.

There was one point in my life when I felt hope, while I was in the Pelletier Department of Youth Services Center. There wasn't much to do but play cards, crochet blankets and talk about how great our street life was; but there was a Bible Study, and I was invited to attend. This was the first time anyone ever showed me the Bible and shared Jesus and the gospel with me. Tina told me about the love of God and that Jesus died for my sins. I couldn't comprehend this at first, yet something in my heart melted that day. She gave me a Bible, which I brought back to my room to read. There wasn't much at that time that could bring tears to my eyes, but there was something about the Bible and the truth that it brought to my heart. I still didn't know what to do with my guilt and shame, but I began to start taking responsibility for my sin and felt sorrow toward God. I developed a fledgling prayer life and would even talk to the other girls about God. I didn't know any other Christians in my life, so when I left, I didn't know how to follow the Bible.

My life of sin and pain progressed. I turned 18 years old in a detention center and when released, I went into a halfway house in Boston, Massachusetts. Downtown, I was approached by a sweet talking guy who swept me off my feet. In a matter of thirty minutes he had convinced me to leave the halfway house and move in with him. When I got to his house. it was a lot different than what he had described. Immediately he asked me to give him all of my personal identification and I gave it to him not thinking anything. There was another girl there, who welcomed me, and reassured me I was making a good decision by being there. We smoked a blunt and within hours she was helping me squeeze into a short, skin-tight dress and giving me a quick lesson on how to "wave" and other instructions on the "dos" and "don'ts" of prostituting. We jumped into a cab to downtown Boston and I was dropped off on a corner. The sweet talking guy who picked me up, that I now knew as my pimp, yelled at me to wave. Everything happened so quickly.

I had never seen anything like it; endless cars driving around in a circle looking for a "date" they could pay for. I waved and ended up getting into a car; I was so scared, but learned the routine quick. That night I gave another piece of my soul away. Sleeping around was nothing new for me. Being promiscuous was something that I did to survive, but now I knew I had entered a whole new world. The rest of the night was kind of a blur; all I remember is taking a cab back to the room when the sun started coming up. This pattern continued for a couple of weeks, until a local drug dealer named John "rescued" me.

John was the type of guy that I was looking for, because he was completely different than my pimp. He convinced me that he would take care of me and I didn't have to be on the street any longer. He wanted me to stay home and become his live-in girlfriend, but this did not turn out as I had hoped. By now I had grown to love the fast life and continued to live that lifestyle on weekends. Things fell apart completely with John and he eventually gave me some crack to sell and told me to leave.

From there I got myself into quite a predicament when I was cornered by three pimps and forced to make a "choice" (to choose a pimp to work for because I couldn't be out there by myself). I was scared, so I quickly chose one of them. He picked me up a bundle of heroin to satisfy my habit and we began "working" in Manhattan immediately. This was by far the scariest thing that I had yet to experience in my life. The stroll where all the prostitutes and pimps were located, was much bigger than the one in Boston. My nights consisted of getting in and out of cars, getting robbed, and experiencing so much perversity, that I became numb to it all and was surprised by nothing. My heart was so hard; I felt completely worthless, run down and broken. This new pimp wouldn't settle for less than a certain amount of money each night. If it wasn't enough, his routine was to question me, search me for extra money, force me to sit on the bed, roll up a blunt, turn the TV volume high and just start punching me all over my body.

> I would cry and beg him to stop,
> eventually the crying stopped and I would just
> wait for him to stop beating me.

New York City was deeply wounding for me; so many bad things had happened, that I didn't think I could ever forget.

I went back to Worcester and started using again. I was arrested and placed in the Massachusetts Correctional Institution (MCI) in Framingham. Through all of these life or death situations, I knew enough to call on God. Whether in the hotel rooms getting beat up by the pimps, or being brought to perverted situations by a trick or being raped at knifepoint, I knew to call on God. I never doubted that He was real. I believe it was only God that kept me alive and rescued me time after time.

Changed Lives

Once released from MCI, I went to a program in Worcester to get "clean" and make some kind of sense out of my life. However, I couldn't follow their rules and was asked to leave. The cycle started again; I could barely believe it, but I ended up back on the streets, looking for heroin and shooting coke. I would use drugs for a couple days straight with no sleep. After a while I couldn't get high anymore. Something (now I know it was the Holy Spirit) was leading me to go to church. I felt very drawn to go to a small Baptist Church off Main Street that a counselor had brought me to before. My appearance must have looked absolutely crazy, but I knew I had to get in there. When I got to the church, the minute I walked in, I felt all of the shame and guilt I had tried cover up. Everyone was praising and dancing. I felt so ashamed I didn't know what to do, but go into the coatroom in the back of the church. I shut the door and began to cry out to God with every part of my soul. I begged Him to forgive me and to help me to stop living the life that I was living. I begged God to let me die or to give me a "Changed Life." I know that day, July 16, 2001, was the day Jesus Christ saved me. My heart was changed and softened and little did I know I had become a new creation (2 Corinthians 5:17).

Though my insides had changed, I certainly didn't look any different. The people of the church prayed for me and then sent me on my way, right back down Main Street. Thankfully this time, I was in God's hands and He did not let me go. I ended up shooting heroin one more time, and woke up in someone's apartment building with a tract on my lap that read, "Do you want Eternal Life?" I knew God was getting my attention, I knew He was speaking to me and it was time to listen. Minutes later, the police came and arrested me for trespassing. I was put in a paddy wagon and taken to jail. I had a six month suspended sentence, so I ended up serving all six months. However, this time in jail it was so much different for me; I had new eyes and ears. The barbed-wire fence that surrounded me, and the constant talk of how "good" the street life was, made me determined to never be a part of that life again. All I could do was surrender to what God was doing in my life, on my knees and broken before Him. I picked up my Bible, cried a lot over my shame and began asking God to forgive me. I felt convicted of sin and actually felt guilt for doing the things that I used to enjoy. My heart was so perverse, but I knew that God was transforming it.

As my jail time was coming to an end, I asked God what to do next. I didn't want to go to another program and try another thing. I knew I wanted to live my life for Him, but I didn't know how to. When I was released from jail on January 2, 2002, I was at the train station and I was undecided about what I should do next. I called the only Christian friend I had, Tina, who had ministered to me in the detention center in Boston. I told her my situation and that I didn't want to go back to the streets of Worcester. She told me to take a train to Boston to meet her. I did, and once I arrived she began to tell me about a fifteen month Christian program called Teen Challenge. I knew right away God had heard my cry for help and once again He was rescuing me.

I called and spoke with the person who first interviewed me and they had told me a little of their story. It was so encouraging. That night, I was accepted into the Providence, Rhode Island Women's Teen Challenge Center, with no money and nothing but the clothes on my back. The minute I walked through the doors, I was welcomed with a hug; I felt the peace that I was looking for my whole life. I soon learned that peace was God's presence. Immediately I felt safe, cared for, and I knew I had finally found refuge.

The program was very difficult, not in the sense of whether to leave or stay, because for I knew right away this was exactly where I was supposed to be. However it was difficult going through the healing process that God was bringing me through. One of the first sermons I heard that completely changed my life, was on forgiveness. The Holy Spirit immediately began to point out the areas in my life where others had hurt me. That night, I wept at an altar before God, begging Him to help me forgive my mother for abandoning me, the pimps who abused me, the men who raped me and finally myself, for all the pain I had self-inflicted. 1 John 1:9 says, "If we confess our sins, he is faithful and just to forgive us our sins and to cleanse us from all unrighteousness." I learned that it was a sin not to forgive others, including myself. At this point being 19 years old, my main goal was to please God. I told Him, He could have my life, I didn't want it anymore. I learned how to trust God through the program and how to submit to authority. I learned how to develop self-discipline, relate to others and build friendships and relationships. I was at a completely new beginning, and I would bring nothing from my past with me. I began talking to my family again and asked them for forgiveness for all I had put them through. Although my dad died a few months later, which was absolutely devastating to me, I was able to reconcile with him and share Jesus with him. I felt that I had wasted so much time because I never allowed my family to get to know me, and I never got to know them. This is still a growing process, even today.

When my time in the program was coming to a close, I began to ask God what should I do with my life. I desperately wanted to be productive and live a life that pleased Him. I didn't have an issue with drugs anymore and I wanted to tell everyone about Jesus. I was given responsibility in Teen Challenge and it felt great to be trusted with other people's lives.

One night during prayer, the Lord spoke to me through John 21:17 - "He said to him the third time, 'Simon, son of

John, do you love me?' Peter was grieved because he said to him the third time, 'Do you love me?' and he said to him, 'Lord, you know everything; you know that I love you.' Jesus said to him, 'Feed my sheep.'"

I knew I loved God, but I didn't know how to show Him my love. Thankfully, it was made clear to me that night.

> He wanted me to share the good news of my freedom from addiction and forgiveness of sin.

The joy I had developed in my heart was priceless. The fact that I could be forgiven and my old life was not held against me, by the Almighty Creator of heaven and earth, was glorious. Nothing could compare to this! All I could do was praise Him. I was completely dead in my sin, and I knew that only God could have called me to that church closet that day, where His goodness and kindness led me to repentance.

Ephesians 2:1-7 says, "You were dead in your sins in which you once walked, following the course of this world, following the prince of the power of the air... but God, being rich in mercy, because of the great love with which he loved us... raised us up with him and seated us with him in the heavenly places in Christ Jesus."

When Teen Challenge hired me in May of 2003, the Lord told me to trust Him. It was a difficult thing for me to learn, since I had no history of trusting anyone or anything. My whole life had been one disappointment after another, but through God's Word (Romans 12:1-2), He began to renew my mind and teach me how to trust Him. I can truly say I have never been disappointed by God.

After a couple of years working at Teen Challenge, I knew He was revealing to me that this was not just a career, but also a calling for me to serve in this ministry full time. I accepted this responsibility with fear and trembling. It was such a joy to live on campus, be around the ladies and share with them the Word of God. During this time I met Jonathan, my husband, who was a graduate of the men's program. While dating Jonathan, God began to reveal another depth of His love to me, because I was very scared when Jonathan expressed his love for me. I never had been in a committed relationship with anyone, and can say that I certainly was never in love with anyone. Those words made me very nervous. Before I could reciprocate them back to him, I knew I had to be ready to love in action, and not just out of emotion. Months later I declared my love to him, he proposed, and we were married on September 2, 2006. What a miracle it was for me to experience a love like this and what a privilege to become his wife.

As of this writing, I have been working at Teen Challenge for 11 years. There have been many trials, victories, and accomplishments along the way. To stay faithful has been the biggest reward of all. To know God is my strength and my satisfaction, has been priceless. I have been able to minister in various different jails, rehabs, and detoxes all over New England and also in Mexico. I have been able to boldly share my testimony of hope and transformation through Jesus Christ alone. I have gained tremendous friendships and relationships through the years like nothing I had ever experienced. While trusting God, He has always done more than I could ask for, think of, or even imagine, for myself. God has always blessed me with the desires of my heart, and if He has said no, He has given me the grace to face and deal with the issue.

I will never forget the sin and the mess that He has rescued me from. I try to remain humble and teachable every day. I currently work as the Admissions Coordinator for the Adult and Teen Challenge Women's Home. I talk to families and women in crisis and help facilitate their Admission process. I am also part of the Kitchen Department; training the students in nutrition and portion control.

Additionally, I work part time at the YMCA as a Fitness Instructor, teaching spin classes. It has been a joy to work in the community and build relationships there. This year I recently passed my Certification as a Personal Trainer with AFAA. I am very excited about this new journey of health and fitness and count it a privilege to train and educate others with goals of becoming healthy. Someday I would like to open my own fitness studio.

As I trust Jesus with my whole life today, I remember my prayer when I was desperate for Him to rescue me out of addiction. I told Him that He could have my life and use it. When I look at what He has given me, the joy and peace I have in my heart; I am in awe of who He is. His faithfulness, His goodness, and His providence are absolutely incredible! I can say I have learned the secret of contentment; delighting myself in Jesus and finding my complete satisfaction in Him alone. I truly have a "Changed Life!"

Chapter 4
Crack Cocaine to Clinical Counselor

Michael Fanjoy

My name is Michael Fanjoy and I am a Teen Challenge New England graduate. This is a story of a "Changed Life" that came about because of the power of Jesus Christ. My story begins like many Teen Challenge students, a difficult childhood and adolescent drug usage. I was raised in a single-parent home in Sanford, Maine and my mother did her best to provide me with all I needed. I was a hyperactive child, often getting into trouble. The first time I was arrested was around the age of thirteen for aiding in a theft. Consequently, I was placed on house arrest for six months. I started using drugs and drinking alcohol around the age of sixteen and this quickly became an important part of my life. As a junior in high school my grades slipped and as a result I no longer could compete in Scholastic sports programs.

After high school my addiction continued to progress. I

was arrested many times and continued to seek more danger-ous drugs and the lifestyle behaviors associated with them. At age twenty-two, my apartment was raided by the Drug Enforcement Administration and I was arrested for cultiva-tion and trafficking of marijuana. At the time, I was dealing marijuana and various hallucinogenic substances, while I was using crystal meth and cocaine. Shortly after this, in the year 2000, I moved to Utah and followed my dream to become a professional snowboarder. While in Utah, I dove further and further into heavy drug addiction, eventually working my way into a Mexican cartel while dealing cocaine on a regular basis.

At this time I learned how to process cocaine into crack, and became a regular user and dealer of crack cocaine.

> I became very lost and consumed with my drug addiction, feeling more worthless every day.

I truly believed there was no way out and this would be my reality for the rest of my life. I became very close with a young woman in Utah and got her hooked on crack cocaine. She and her family cared for me very much and overlooked my behavior as I manipulated them and everyone else I came in contact with. We were living in a crack house and had been smoking crack cocaine every day for a year when I ended up getting her pregnant. She was five months into the pregnancy and weighed 80 pounds. We believed our only option in this circumstance was an abortion, and she went through with the procedure. Often people do not think of the long-term consequences of their decisions; this one will bring me tears for the rest of my life.

After a very dangerous situation occurred while dealing with the Mexican cartel, I fled Utah with the help of my mother and moved back to Maine. This was the first time I admitted to my mother and family that I had a problem with drugs and alcohol. For the next few years, my family tried to intervene in any way they could to help me with my drug problem. However, I continued to do whatever I could to get and use crack cocaine and other drugs.

My mother would often find me in the basement of her house "all cracked out" and looking like death. I owed many drug dealers money. One time they came to my mother's house with a shotgun looking for me. I started to steal money from my mother and pawned her gold and diamond jewelry for drugs. My mother called the police on me several times, not knowing what else to do. She eventually changed the locks on the doors so I could not get back in. In the last year of my active drug use, I moved into a crack house. I started sharing needles to take heroin, in order to come down from the crack binges. I was surrounded by death and desperation set in. I did not care to live anymore and my behavior became more careless, dangerous, and reckless every day.

I was truly lost and felt very lonely, empty, and hopeless. It was at this time, on a three-day crack binge, at two in the morning, that God first spoke to me. Three other people and I decided to rob one of the local drug distributors. We stole their safe and broke it open with a sledgehammer. We found a pound of crack cocaine, money and a bottle of Klonopin. We split the piles of crack among us and smoked it for three days straight. Unbeknownst to me, this would be my last time using drugs. On the third day of smoking crack, at two in the morning, I was sitting out on the porch feeling like ending it all.

> Then, a still small voice spoke to me and said that this will be the last time I was going to smoke crack and He would take care of me.

I did not realize until later that this was Jesus speaking directly to me.

In November of 2003 at a prayer meeting, my sister learned about Teen Challenge New Hampshire and God intervened and helped me to get into the program. I arrived in Manchester where the house supervisor, greeted my sister and me. I hadn't showered for a week, was 50 pounds underweight, and had just come off a three-day crack and heroin binge. The house supervisor wanted me to go to the hospital for detoxification, but my sister insisted I stay. I was sick and slept for three days while I detoxified from the drugs, and finally came down. When I started to feel better, I met some amazing men at Teen Challenge and turned my life over to Jesus Christ.

Going through the early phases in Teen Challenge was a very difficult process for me. I was depressed, had a very negative attitude and behaved poorly towards the staff. I had difficulty with the curriculum, scripture memorization and was often placed on restriction. I got through this tough time only by focusing on the teachings of Jesus and His amazing grace. I also connected with the other students in the house and we became very supportive of and close to one another. In my second month of the program I was privileged to greet a new student at the front gate coming into the Teen Challenge program. This young man was jaundiced, coming off of heroin and facing federal prosecution for murder. Jesus did an amazing work in this student's life and it was memorable for me, because he was the first person in whom I witnessed a powerful and miraculous transformation from death to life. He soon became one of my best friends and eventually the best man in my wedding. He continues to be instrumental in my life today.

During my stay at Teen Challenge I traveled with the choir, often sharing my testimony in churches from Vermont to Maine. I watched many people give their lives to Christ and witnessed His transformative power over and over again. I became better at scripture memorization and worked my way through the Bible along with the student curriculum. I eventually worked my way through the phases of the program and traveled to the Teen Challenge New England Training Center in Brockton, Massachusetts. During this phase my studies were intensified. I worked in the kitchen during my whole stay at Brockton. I participated as the administrative "white house" server and was on the traveling catering crew. I spent a lot of time in the kitchen serving the men. I grew very close with the other kitchen staff; they were truly like brothers. At times the kitchen was a very difficult place to be. I would wake up at 5 am, before anyone else in the house, to start preparing the day's meals. Then I would usually be the last one to bed, because I was either cleaning up, preparing late night meals or prepping food for the following day.

> I now can see how God used this ministry
> to stretch me and strengthen my character
> to be the man I am today.

While at the Brockton Training Center I truly learned the concept of Proverbs 27:17 "As iron sharpens iron, so one person sharpens another".

Halfway through my stay at Teen Challenge, God spoke

and told me that I would never go back to my old life and that he had a lot of work for me to do. At this time I wasn't sure what He had in mind, but I started to think about college. I did not believe I would get accepted because my cognitive ability was so poor. Little did I know that God's grace would prevail, and I would be accepted to Valley Forge Christian College (VFCC) in Pennsylvania. It was so far from home and the idea of studying in college was very overwhelming. I believed God called me nonetheless, and as Paul said in 2 Corinthians 5:7 "For we walk by faith and not by sight" I accepted His calling and enrolled in VFCC.

While at VFCC, I remained focused on God's call on my life and became very passionate in my studies. God placed me with an amazing roommate who was also passionately following the call of God on his life. I connected with other Teen Challenge graduates on campus and we gave each other strength to get through this difficult time of study. I also participated in a lot of campus and student ministries and even became the leader for the Teen Challenge ministry "Keeping it Real." While I was a part of this ministry, I led a team who traveled to Philadelphia and Pennsylvania Teen Challenge's training center, "God's Mountain" in Rehrersburg, Pennsylvania. I led the chapel services and our team shared testimonies of hope to the hopeless.

At VFCC, I was also a Resident Assistant leader for

my dorm for two years and was involved in a campus men's group called, "Iron Sharpens Iron." My walk with God grew very strong during my time at VFCC and I truly learned the principles of 2 Timothy 3:16-17 "All Scripture is given by inspiration of God, and is profitable for doctrine, for reproof, for correction, for instruction in righteousness, that the man of God may be complete, thoroughly equipped for every good work." I obtained a Bachelor of Science in Psychology with a minor in pastoral counseling at VFCC, but God did not stop there. I also met my beautiful wife Danae, and married her right there in the campus chapel! During our time at college, God spoke of His intention for graduate school to my wife and I. After VFCC, Danae and I enrolled in the Immaculata University's Masters in Counseling Psychology program. At this time, I also accepted a position as a primary clinical counselor at a residential rehabilitation program. While working at a state licensed clinical rehabilitation program, I obtained my certification as a drug and alcohol counselor through the Pennsylvania Department of Health. After three years of work at this rehabilitation center, I accepted a position at an outpatient clinic, which helps people with addiction transition from a residential setting back home to their families and communities.

Currently, I am part of a Christian counseling program employed as a Christian counselor and facilitating intensive outpatient group sessions, as a part of a reentry program.

I am also the site director and clinical supervisor for the outpatient counseling clinic in Exton, Pennsylvania. Danae and I are scheduled to graduate with our Master's degrees from Immaculata University in August 2014. I am currently in supervision and on track to earn my license as a professional counselor in 2016. Danae is pregnant with our second son and our family continues to seek God's guidance and direction. Last November, I celebrated ten years of my walk with God and freedom from the bondage of drugs and alcohol. Everyday I feel immensely blessed to witness God's amazing grace in my life and in the lives of those who receive this free gift. I can stand with confidence in Christ and proclaim that I have gone from **addiction** to **freedom** and now live a "Changed Life."

"... for God's gifts and His call are irrevocable. Just as you who were at one time disobedient to God have now received mercy as a result of their disobedience, so they too have now become disobedient in order that they too may now receive mercy as a result of God's mercy to you. For God has bound everyone over to disobedience so that he may have mercy on them all." Romans 11:29-32

Chapter 5
From The Inside Out

Ronald Charles

My family lived in poverty and went through many difficult times. There was never enough food to eat or proper clothing to wear. We had just barely enough to survive. My single mother did the best she could with her six children. Unfortunately, my father never had any concern with or involvement in my life. At a young age I began stealing, lying and skipping school because it seemed to have no value to me. I looked up to the older boys on the street and by twelve years old I began smoking marijuana and drinking with them. Before long I was on a road to destruction that included stealing cars and robbing the local corner stores. I eventually graduated from using soft drugs to crack cocaine, which quickly became my drug of choice.

My love for crack cocaine was so great that it blinded me from seeing the true value of my first marriage. I caused my wife so much pain and suffering that when she couldn't take it anymore, she filed for a divorce. My family tried numerous times to get me help, but I was in deep denial thinking I could handle it and stop whenever I wanted to.

Years later, when I was 36 years old a young woman named Susan came into my life, impacting it forever. We both believed in God, but neither of us had a personal relationship with Him. She was from a Catholic background and my upbringing was Protestant. Within a couple of months we were living together. She had no clue that I was a man who had sold his soul to the devil for the drug I desired so much. However, it wasn't long before she learned about my addiction, when I didn't come home one night due to drinking, gambling and drugs. I remember Susan telling me that we could get through anything and that she would help me get free, but my addiction and the lies got worse by the minute. I was spending so much money on drugs that we were unable to pay our bills and became homeless. With too much pride to go to a shelter, we slept in cars in the middle of winter and took showers at my mother's house. Still, Susan was determined not to leave me.

Over time, we had to leave four different apartments due to my addiction. Then for the first time, Susan was dragged into my world of addiction and both our lives were spinning out of control. We had no direction and no hope of living.

Three years later, Susan entered a Teen Challenge

program for a short time and because I missed her so much, my drug use worsened. When she returned from Teen Challenge, she seemed to have a light inside of her, and I wanted it too, desperately. She began to share about life in God that Teen Challenge had taught her, but instead of accepting it, I drew her away from the light back into the dark fiery pits with me.

My addiction had become a two thousand dollars a week habit, so we moved from Danbury to Waterbury into a cheaper place that she could afford, without having to depend on me. There, Susan got so upset with me I finally turned to a small church for help. For the next two years things were somewhat better but I was at a plateau.

Although I was still straddling the fence, Susan thought I was doing better and in 2003 we were officially married. Sadly, the very next day after the wedding I left for work and didn't return home for two days. I went through all the money gifts we had received.

> A couple of years later when Susan
> was pregnant with our first child,
> I went on another binge, leaving her with no car,
> no money or food in the house.

While intoxicated with alcohol and drugs, I broke into and vandalized my workplace. A silent alarm dispatched the police and I was arrested. I was facing ten years in prison but ended up with three years probation, suspended after ten years. Although it seemed pointless, I knew I had to stay clean. One mistake and I could go to prison for up to ten years.

I managed to stay out of trouble for next three years. This was a good time for our family. We had our daughter, Ariyah Destinee Charles, we bought a nice condo in a good area, two cars and had everything we needed. We even sat down for dinner together as a family. I wasn't doing drugs at this time, but the desire never left and the problem still needed to be dealt with.

As soon as my probation ended, I went back to drugs and in less than a year. I lost everything we had worked so hard for. We had to live with my sister and were considering divorce. Then we found out Susan was pregnant with our second child and in 2005, my son Ronnie Louis Charles Jr. was born. Susan stayed home and I worked two full time jobs to pay the bills. I thought that being so busy would help me to stop my addiction, but unfortunately that wasn't the case.

Ronnie Jr. had a lot of problems when he was born and at times Susan would be up for 72 hours straight with him while I did nothing to help her. I couldn't deal with a crying child. Reality was hitting me in the face full force, but I couldn't grasp the concept. My wife was tired and wanted better and

I couldn't blame her. I wanted her to be happy but I couldn't help her. I never showed her love or appreciation. She tried to go back to school, raise our children and live life the right way, but all I did was hold her back. It was like crabs in a bucket: if one tries to get out the others grab that one and pull it right back down.

Finally, Susan threw me out for spending all the money for the bills on drugs. I had to sleep in my car and go to work. During this time, I became very sick from a diabetic coma and was rushed to the hospital. Susan came every day to see me. She took the vows "in sickness and in health" seriously. She took me back into the house and looked past our differences to take care of me until I got well. I promised her that I would get my life right and we would be okay, but that didn't happen.

When Ronnie Jr. was six months old, Susan kicked me out, got a smaller apartment, and began seeing other men to fill her void of affection. Soon, one man moved in and Susan started drinking every weekend. I was doing so poorly this didn't affect me the way it should have, although I made sure I saw the children on weekends.

Years later, I moved back in with her as a roommate to help with the bills. My son was diagnosed with severe ADHD, we lived in a drug infested ghetto area and were both collecting unemployment. The addiction and the fighting between us grew so bad that when the cops were called in, I left. When I returned a few hours later, she gave me an ultimatum to get help or return to the street. If I chose the street, I would not be able to have contact with my children. I agreed to go away for help, not knowing how long I would be gone. Every inpatient rehabilitation center she called would not take me because I had no insurance. I now know this was God's plan. Since she knew of Teen Challenge, she called them and reached someone in Vermont who would talk to me.

> Broken and destroyed, I explained that
> I needed help and couldn't take it anymore.

The next day the decision was made and I was going to Teen Challenge in Vermont. They accepted me with no money, no insurance and completely broken. I was nervous because I never travelled anywhere and now I was driving three hours away from the city to a place where I knew no one. The placement in Vermont was necessary, to be far enough from home so I couldn't leave. I had to be separated from the outside world in order to realize the life I had created was destroying me and others. My family and I arrived at Teen Challenge late at night. The staff greeted me and I was searched for any items I wasn't allowed to have. I kissed my family goodbye, and then they were gone.

I knew this was not going to be an easy road. I had to

follow rules and take orders from others, which I lacked the discipline for. But I knew that my wife wasn't going to change her mind about our agreement. My plans consisted getting clean to making her happy, but something else happened in Vermont. **I found God!** I stayed in Vermont for thirty days. Then, thankfully, Pastor Rick Welch made it possible for me to be transferred to New Haven Teen Challenge, enabling me to be visited by my family.

After working so hard for those thirty days, I received my first blessing. While I was in Teen Challenge, my family back home was not doing well. Susan was drinking a lot and had a new man in her life who was not a good influence. Things were spiraling out of control and I wanted to go home. My wife was faced with a DCF case because of her drinking. I prayed that she would be delivered and my children would be fine. I thank God that the DCF investigation was a closed case thirty days later.

Because Susan was seeing someone else, the possibility that we may never be together again hurt me. After almost two months when my family came to visit me, I asked her to put our family back together again.

Susan went through more difficulties while I was in the Teen Challenge Program. I wanted to go back and help her, but my mentor, Mike Hayes, explained to me that God was looking over my family and I must trust in Him in order for

Changed Lives

God's work to continue in me. I prayed that God would watch over them, take care of them and meet all of their needs. At times, all I wanted was to leave, but Teen Challenge was where I needed to be. Finally Susan confirmed that we could be together again, though both of us knew that it would be a hard road because we had been apart for more than four years.

> When Susan came to visit me she saw the transformation that was happening in my life and it caused her to start to go to church with the kids.

They never missed a visit, which was a three hour train ride. They walked to the train station in the rain, sleet, snow and sunshine to be there. They were jumping through hoops to make it a point to show me that they loved me and were in my corner. When the visits were over, my kids would encourage me by saying, "Daddy stay in the program. We love you." My children knew that I needed to be there to get right with everything. Susan also let God transform her while she worked hard to register and insure the cars, hold a job, take care of the children and even quit drinking.

Today we live in a clean, quiet, three-bedroom apartment on the outskirts of Waterbury, Connecticut. God has called us to stay and help others in our community. I have a good job with the great help of Teen Challenge. When I was having my home visits, I attended the church that my family loved. I soon realized that this was the church I wanted to attend when I graduated from Teen Challenge. We are working closely with Pastor Jose for a strong, Christian marriage. We are learning how to raise our children on a Christian foundation. They attend the church, Missionettes and Royal Rangers programs. No matter how tough things got for her, Susan always told me to stay in Teen Challenge. Where I was weak, she was strong and where she was weak, I was strong. Recently, my wife was diagnosed with lupus. We both know that God didn't clean us up for nothing and God can do the impossible when we have faith.

I would like to thank Teen Challenge for changing me from the inside out. Teen Challenge teaches discipline and structure that can be carried on for life. It doesn't just clean you up. It transforms your life into a personal relationship with God. Pastor Rick, Sister Edith, Pastor Jose and Mike Hayes have all been an inspiration in my life. They did God's work and helped me find God. Teen Challenge prepared me for the outside world's battle. While in the program, I thought that some rules were not good, but soon I realized that every rule would prepare me to stay humble, have accountability for my whereabouts and know how to behave towards others.

I can't express how grateful I am to Teen Challenge for all the help transitioning back home. In the summer of 2014,

Changed Lives

I returned to my family and started a new chapter in my life. The story is not over, it has just begun. God's work in our lives is never complete.

My story had to be told in order for people to know that I was an extreme addict and God cleaned me up. I am now free from addiction and no longer bound by the worldly demons of life. Now I want to pass along the blessing that I received to others who may desperately need help. This scripture has been key in my "Changed Life": "For I know the plans I have for you, declares the Lord, plans to prosper you and not to harm you, plans to give you hope and future." Jeremiah 29:11

I truly thank God for giving me the strength to overcome the power of addiction and giving me a "Changed Life."

Chapter 6
A Life of Emptiness to Abundance

Jenny McCaffrey

This is the story of my journey from a life of emptiness to a life of abundance. My name is Jenny McCaffrey and I was raised in central New Jersey. Growing up I had two loving parents, Michael and Janice McCaffrey, and three older brothers Michael, Mark and Shawn. I grew up in a household where my father was the provider and my mother was the nurturer. My parents did everything possible to show me what the right direction for my life should be. My father worked a lot and was always gone; therefore he played a very small role in my life. Unfortunately, I remember fear entering my heart at a very young age.

I was in second grade when we picked up everything and moved to Florida to care for my dying grandfather. A lot of problems arose when we moved there. My brother Mark was badly influenced by a gang and drugs. My brother Shawn's

good friend was accidentally shot and killed. When my grandfather passed away, my parents decided we would move back
to Toms River, New Jersey where the rest of our family was.

I was in the fifth grade when I began to experience
the chaos from the arguing and fighting all around me. I did
not understand it and at times I would cry because I was so
scared of the fighting between my father and my brother. I
never knew what to expect, so I learned to put a smile on my
face and pretend like everything was okay. My mother tried to
shelter me from these domestic issues.

I got involved with soccer, basketball and softball. I
loved playing sports and they became a big part of my life.
My brother's friends started calling me "Butch" because of the
way I dressed and acting like a tomboy. I hated being called
that name because I already had low self-esteem and I did not
feel pretty.

We picked up and moved once again to Jackson, New
Jersey when I was in the eighth grade. That year I became
more "girly" and sought the attention of boys. I desired to have
someone pay attention to me and love me because my dad
never did. I began searching for love in all the wrong places.
When my first boyfriend Matt broke up with me, the pain was
so strong and heartbreaking, I wondered why and what was
wrong with me. I felt I wasn't good enough. That was the summer I began drinking and smoking weed in a park in Jack-

son. That was where I found freedom and confidence and it seemed all the fear I felt was gone.

Unfortunately, all my problems were still there. I was 13 years old and this was the beginning of my ten-year journey of addiction to drugs and alcohol. I soon progressed to drinking and using ecstasy every weekend while partying with older guys. I was sixteen years old when I got a fake ID which opened the door for me to go to the bars to drink and party.

By the eleventh grade I had a serious drinking problem and cocaine addiction. I would visit several nightclubs from Atlantic City to New York City. I was doing all kinds of drugs: cocaine, ecstasy, pills, kay, and crystal meth. The day I realized things were really bad was when I became physically sick from using prescription Percocet and Oxycontin. My reaction to this was to begin taking more to build up my tolerance.

I was in love with the party scene. I was one person during the day and a different person at night. I seemed to not have a care in the world because I had no feelings at all, but the more I partied, the more guilt and shame was produced from my lifestyle. Every morning, I woke up feeling terrible, hating the way I had acted, and hating the way I treated people, including myself, the night before. I started to lose all self-worth and self-respect. All I wanted was someone to love me, but I didn't love myself or care about myself, so I allowed men to use me.

My security was in an outward façade of wearing the best clothes and my hair always looking just right. If my outside appearance looked good, I felt good and believed others would like me. Soon I met a guy who was dealing drugs and we became inseparable. I thought we had fallen in love. He had some money saved up, so after six months we decided to move in together. While living together he introduced me to heroin. We started sniffing it at first, and then went right to smoking crack. I had tried smoking crack a few times before, but it never became a habit. However, this time it became an everyday habit. Its addictive quality was frightening to me.

My boyfriend became very abusive and I was stuck in a spiral of craziness. We started going to a methadone clinic, tried Alcoholics and Narcotics Anonymous meetings, clinics, suboxone (an opiate treatment) and a counselor; but nothing worked. I was so depressed and felt so far away from reality. Every morning I would wake up, look into the mirror and I hate the person I saw. I was once a little girl who had dreams to be great, but now my life was completely destroyed by drugs with no way out. Everything I said I would never do, I did.

When I was 23 years old, I started using needles and robbing anyone who came across my path. Life couldn't have gotten any worse for me. One of our family members named Danielle, died at 19 years old from a drug abuse infection. Even when I was at her funeral, I was using heroin in the bathroom. However, when I looked at her corpse in the casket, I became terrified that I might die.

Soon after that funeral, my boyfriend and I went on a vacation with my mom, dad and brother to Sea World in Florida. The whole theme at Sea World was "Believe" but I did not have one ounce of faith inside me to believe that my life would ever get better. One night during that vacation I told my brother everything I was doing and that I didn't want to live like that anymore.

> I told him how I felt like I wanted to die inside and that I couldn't take the pain anymore.

It got so bad I blacked out and the next morning when I awoke, my parents asked me if I was ready to get help. I remember that day like it was yesterday. I was ready to get help but also afraid to go even one day without drugs.

When we got back home, my parents made a lot of phone calls, but there were no places that would take me without insurance. While returning back to their house from yet another place that denied me, my dad's phone rang and a Pastor named Dino asked how I was doing. He told us not to worry and told me about a place called Teen Challenge and their Providence, Rhode Island Women's Home. We got the phone number and I called to inquire about the program.

I asked if I could smoke cigarettes and if my boyfriend could come visit me there. After hearing no to both questions, I hung up the phone and said that was not the place for me and instead I went into a local detox that week. During detox I had to talk to a counselor to discuss where I would be going and I told him about Teen Challenge and how I didn't want to go. He told me, "You are going to go to this place because it is going to change your life." I didn't understand anything he was saying, but went to sleep that night and awoke to peace in my heart about going there. I believe God used that counselor to guide me to Teen Challenge. Once I walked through their doors and right up until today, five years later, I never craved a cigarette again. I used to smoke two packs a day. Miracles like this started happening to me right before my eyes. I felt the love of God, the very thing I was searching for my whole life. People I hardly knew were showing me this love that I could not explain. I didn't sleep for two and a half weeks, but Lisa Smith, one of the staff members, stayed up with me every night until I was okay. She poured out her heart and talked with me.

Two weeks into the program we visited a Bible college. There they had a special exhibit and we walked through and saw reenactments of human trafficking, child soldiers and starving children in other countries. I began to cry as if my eyes were open for the first time and I could see the pain around the world. I saw life in a new way that night. Previously I was so self-consumed and never cared about anyone else. During the worship service and the Word of God, my heart was touched so much and once again, I cried. My life had been so selfish, dark and separated from God.

> That night I was rescued and found hope as I accepted Jesus Christ as Lord and Savior.

For two months I cried every day because of my feelings of guilt and shame. I asked the Lord to forgive me for what I did to others and myself, and He did. 1 John 1:9 says, "But if we confess our sins to him, he is faithful and just to forgive us from our sins and to cleanse us from all wickedness." I felt His forgiveness and freedom. A huge weight was lifted off me.

I wanted to know more about God and on April 23, 2009 I decided after 30 days in Teen Challenge that I wanted to get baptized and finish the whole fifteen and a half month program. I realized that I had lived with years of pain and needed to take time to allow God to heal my heart. I was amazed at God's love for me.

I began to pray and read the Bible and learned in Ephesians 2:4-5 that it says, "Because of His great love for us, God who is rich in mercy, made us alive with Christ even when we were dead in our sin. It is by grace you have been saved." I realized that God loved me before I even knew Him. Even if I was a mess and dirty, He would love me the same, even if I didn't change a thing. It was His love that melted my heart and things began to change. I realized I didn't curse anymore. My heart became more willing and softer to do the things that pleased God.

For one year straight my prayer was, "God let me love the things you love and hate the things you hate." My rebellious lifestyle had been the complete opposite of the Word of God. There was a lot of healing and issues that had to be worked out. God answered my prayer and changed my heart and desires. My whole perspective changed and I knew my life would never be the same again.

I do and always will thank God for Teen Challenge and the two and a half years I spent there. I am the woman I am today because of Teen Challenge. Teen Challenge produced a lot of character in me. I once had no discipline or structure in my life, but because of the program I learned how to submit and surrender to God and leadership. Today when I face trials or hard circumstances, I know how to turn to God and pray. Now I ask for advice and guidance before making a decision. I have never been so free in my life. I have found true peace and freedom come only from Jesus Christ. I can say with confidence that I have been set free from my addiction.

Two scriptures I love are 2 Corinthians 5:17 "Therefore, if anyone is in Christ, he is a new creation; the old is gone, the new has come." I know my old past is no longer a part of my life. With God I have a new future filled with love, joy, and peace. The second scripture is 2 Corinthians 3:17, "Where the spirit of the Lord is there is freedom." I now know there is freedom every day in the Word of God. There is peace even if everything around me seems to be falling apart.

After finishing the program at Teen Challenge, I remained as a staff member for a year and a half. During that time I found out who I, Jenny, really was. I was able to share with other women all that was freely given to me. It is amazing to share the love of God with others. During that time, God helped me overcome a lot of fears and insecurities. I ran the fundraising department and once a month preached sermons to the women in the program, helping me overcome my fear of public speaking. On my day off, I began going to the streets with my friend Megan Kite to talk with the homeless and give them hope. God then breathed a passion in my heart for the homeless and people in need. I share with others who are suffering from drugs and alcohol addiction and let them know there is hope.

God has turned my whole family around for good. My mom, dad, brother Shawn, his wife Kaylen, and I all go to church together. My relationship with my mom and dad is growing. My dad and I now spend quality time together as we finish our second year of Bible school together! My brothers Shawn and Mark are also now free from drugs and serving the Lord. My relationship with my brother Michael is growing and I pray that he and his wife will also come to know Jesus.

I attend Spanish bi-lingual Missionary Pentecostal Church in Lakewood, New Jersey. I don't speak the language, but I know I am right where I belong. Pastor Hector Salugero also attended Teen Challenge in Puerto Rico over 40 years ago, so I feel right at home. I help at their soup kitchen for the homeless each week and serve in many areas of the church. Teen Challenge taught me to surround myself with good people who were stronger in their faith than me. Pastor Hector and Raquel Salugero are like my spiritual parents. In March of 2013, we went on a missionary trip to Dominican Republic. There I celebrated four years clean and sober and got to share my story. We visited the five planted churches of Missionary Pentecostal Church and encouraged them. It amazed me how much less the people have there, yet they are filled with so much love. It was such a blessing for me to give of myself to others in need.

Of course I had some adjustments when I came home and I went through a period of loneliness. I realize life will always have its struggles.

I also know my worst day with Jesus is still better than my best day before He came into my life.

I believe the most important thing is to have an intimate relationship with Jesus.

I want God to flourish in every area of my life and by His grace I am not going to settle for anything but the best He has for me, because in my past, I never thought my life would amount to anything. Once I left Teen Challenge, I finally got my cosmetology license, which I failed at four times during my addiction years. Praise God, I can do all things through Christ who gives me strength! About a year and a half later the opportunity of a lifetime came my way when I got a job at Salon Concrete. There I received advanced training, learning the best techniques from the Vidal Sassoon Academy. I found a gift that God has given me and I am living my passion as I make others feel good about themselves.

Now and then I go back to visit my Teen Challenge home. I tell the new women in the program that it is possible to have a "Changed Life" in Christ. Teen Challenge is where my heart and life was forever changed. I pray that every drug addict would know and hear about the love and freedom of Jesus Christ. I also pray that one day we will have a Women's Teen Challenge home in New Jersey and I can be a part of it. Five years later, I give God all the glory and honor for my "Changed Life!"

Chapter 7
Bankrupt & Homeless

Thomas Parker

I still remember the day when I was 13 years old and my life fell apart. I grew up in a lower income neighborhood in Boston, Massachusetts where my father was a house painter. I was sitting in class at Catholic grammar school, when there was a knock at the door. The nun opened the door, and another, older nun was standing out in hallway, looking very serious. The nuns whispered to each other, and then motioned toward me.

"What did I do now?" I thought. I wasn't a bad kid, although I did get into trouble once in a while. "Come with me, Tommy," the older nun said, and I began following her down the hall. "What's going on?" I asked. She hesitated, then stopped and faced me. "I'm sorry, Tommy. Your mother sent a neighbor here to take you home. She's down the hall in the office. Your father died today, at work."

Changed Lives

I'd always been close to my father. He would come home exhausted from work every night, so we never spent much time together, but he believed in me. He had dreams for me. "You're going to make it, Tom," he'd say. "I didn't get to finish grammar school, but you're going to college. I want you to have the chance that I never had." My father was a marine in WWII and was wounded on Saipan and Iwo Jima. He came home after the war with a serious heart condition. When he went to work that morning, I never saw him alive again. He died instantly of a massive heart attack on the job. He was 47 years old.

I was crushed. A million thoughts went through my head. What happened to him? What about Ma—how would she handle this?

At home, Ma was frantic. I remember walking in the door and she grabbed me and kept saying, "Tommy, what are we going to do?" I felt empty inside. With this one event, my life was up-ended. I would soon find out that I was on my own and that things were going to get much, much worse.

Making My Own Way

Ma and I went to the funeral parlor to pick out a casket. We could barely afford even the cheapest one. Right after my father's funeral, Ma began drinking. We both had to start working. She got a full-time job in the mailroom of a local hospital for minimum wage, and I went to work at a gas station at night, pumping gas to help her with the bills. She was a hard worker, but when she came in the door after work, the bottle became her comfort. Essentially, our life stopped. We were in two different worlds. She still had her friends in the neighborhood, but I was alone and didn't even know it.

As Ma buried herself in her job and drinking at night, our relationship disintegrated. There was no extended family at all, so there was no one to question her about her drinking habits. Besides, she wasn't alone, everyone in the neighborhood drank. There was no one to keep an eye out for me. Home became a place to grab food and to sleep, nothing else. Looking back now, I can understand that Ma's despair was exactly like mine, except I was a young boy growing up very fast.

I started hanging out on the streets, in the bar rooms and in the neighborhood pool halls.

> There, I met all kinds of people—mostly a lot of kids like me, from broken homes, who were always looking for trouble.

I got to know the local hoods, dope-fiends and dealers. This dark subculture excited me, and as I listened to their crime stories, I saw for myself just how crooked the world was. As far as they were concerned, corruption was a way of life. Right away, these guys were my role models and I looked up to them. I fit right in, and they began to take me under their wing.

I was 14 years old when I was caught for my first felony, grand theft auto. I had already been stealing cars for several months, but because I was so young, they let me off with seven months suspended sentence. Now I had a record and with it, the beginning of a reputation. Now I was really in. After that, it was an endless road of arrests and juvenile facilities. I wasn't so lucky anymore to get off with only suspended sentences and probation. I would be in and out of courts, jails, the state hospital and drug programs for the next eighteen years.

When I was 15 years old, I got into drugs. Then, I started "cold-shaking" and "shooting" sleeping pills. What a rush! It was like getting hit by a freight train. At home, Ma would scream and yell at me. I'd yell back then go to bed, leaving her to drink. Who needed her anyway? I didn't need anybody. As long as people just stayed off my back and out of my face, I felt I could do just fine on my own.

Something's Got A Hold of Me

When I woke up in the Boston State Hospital in Mattapan, I was a little confused. Where was I? As my head cleared, it came back to me that I had been shooting up pills the night before. I didn't find out until later, but I had begun to go into a coma in my bed that night while I slept. I remember

Ma hitting me over the head with an old suitcase and telling me to get out. She had found an empty bottle of pills in my jacket pocket. I don't remember too much after that, but some friends of mine said they saw me "crawling" up the highway towards the Catholic church. I made it to the doorstep and passed out. A priest put me in a cab and took me to the hospital. The doctors came out to the cab and said I was too far-gone and couldn't be saved. They wouldn't treat me. Then the priest opened the cab door, grabbed me by the ankles and pulled me out onto the sidewalk. He told them, "Ok, now I'm going to call the local newspaper reporters and have them come and take pictures of this kid dying in front of your hospital because you wouldn't take him in." I guess the doctors got scared and admitted me. Later, I'd wonder if God had stepped in and saved my life.

I was sent to State Hospital for observation, and my stay there accomplished nothing. The doctors asked me why was I doing drugs and I didn't know how answer to that. All I knew was I hated the world and everyone in it.

I knew in my gut that I was destined for some hard, hard times. This was my world: Mom would come home from work and drink until the time she went to bed. We'd fight and she'd look at me with empty hopelessness in her eyes. I couldn't stand that look. Sometimes I would have to carry her upstairs to her bed. Other times I would shut myself in my room, until we'd start the same mess over the next day. When I would reach my boiling point, I'd leave for days at a time and go live with friends.

By now, at 16 years old, I was committing crimes every day, breaking and entering, robberies and drug sales. When I wasn't in school—which was a lot of the time now—I was out on streets stealing and doping. I would get caught and be sent to some juvenile facility. One time in court I tried to get into the service with Ma's signature rather than go back to jail, but the judge told her, "I'm sorry, Mrs. Parker, we already have enough junkies in Vietnam."

By 1967, heroin seemed to take the streets of Boston by storm. It had been there for a long time, but was mainly associated with an underground of hardcore users. Suddenly, it was the drug of the new rock n' roll, free love culture. Even middle and upper class kids from out of town were shooting up. Everyone was doing drugs! The first time I shot heroin into my arm I knew I had found what I had been looking for. This drug was it for me. I was hooked mentally and shortly thereafter, physically!

To this day I have no clue how I got through high school. I was committing crimes and getting high every day. I was expelled from two high schools and barely made it through the third. I wasn't stupid, I just hated school. Of course, spending time in juvenile facilities did slow the process down. I remember when I was released on my 17th birthday I thought, "These guys are not so bad after all. They let me out on my birthday". It was only later I found out that they had to let me out because I was 17 years old and no longer considered a juvenile. I finally managed to graduate, but that's when it started going downhill even faster.

I had no skills, no future, no plans and no one to help me. Not one thing or no one. I was becoming an adult and a new world was opening up to me. I was being introduced to new connections, hitting the downtown nightclubs and running around all the Boston neighborhoods. I was always breaking the law, and always in trouble.

For the next several years, the only things I cared about were drugs and crime. Heroin was now my life. To support my lifestyle, I got even deeper into committing crimes to get drug money. I never thought about my future. Who cares what I do with my life? Only the police and my parole officer cared about my activities. My probation was always extended because I was constantly in trouble.

When I was 18 years old I was sentenced to the drug addiction unit at the State Hospital again.

The following year I got arrested for possession of heroin, and did a year in the House of Corrections.

Changed Lives

When I was released at the end of 1970, I rode the bus back home to my old neighborhood. Reentering the free world was hard for me. Incarceration had affected me mentally. As I looked out the window, I reflected on my time behind bars as a juvenile and now as an adult. I had been miserable without my freedom and I swore to myself that I would never go back again. When the bus got to my stop, I stepped off thinking, there's no way I'm going back on dope. Then suddenly I heard, "Hey, Tommy!" I turned my head. What a weird coincidence. There was a neighborhood dealer I grew up with who had been one of my cellmates. "Come over to my place", he said, "I got a free shot for you to celebrate getting out." Twenty minutes later I was wrapping a belt around my arm, thinking, "You're nuts, Tommy. You've been locked up for a year and you just promised yourself you'd go straight." But I was absolutely powerless to resist. The first chance I got, I was back in the "jackpot" again: that's heroin!

Within one day of getting out of jail, I was right back on heroin. Plunging the needle in my vein I thought, who cares? But then something happened that I thought might change my life. I ran into an old girlfriend of mine from the neighborhood. She used to give Ma letters to sneak in to me when I was locked up as a juvenile. I saw her on the street one day and we seemed to hit it off all over again. Now I wanted to get a job, settle down and go straight. Imagine that!

Bankrupt & Homeless

When I was 23 years old, we got married. I was still on parole of course, but I settled down a bit, got a job, and tried to become a decent guy. Without an education, and no union connections, there were no good jobs open to me. I was working in a machine shop in South Boston in the parts room trying to learn whatever I could. The owners really liked me and I thought that maybe I could learn to be a machinist. They even paid for me to take night school courses working at a college machine shop. I had found a job, but the old-timers were very secretive about their trade. They made sure to never give away their trade secrets for fear that they would lose their job to a younger guy. When I would walk over to a guy to ask a question, he'd put his tools down so I couldn't see how he was doing his work.

Even with nobody rooting for me, I began to want to do something with my life. I got up at 5:00 a.m. to punch in at work by 7:00 a.m. and worked until 5:00 p.m. Then I left work and went straight to school three nights a week. I wouldn't get home until after 11:00 p.m. Because I was banned from holding a driver's license, I had to take the subway and buses to get around. It was a long, hard grind. Ironically, I started drinking every night after work, just like Ma. After a few years, it really started to catch up with me. I knew I couldn't drink like that anymore, so I did the only other thing I could; I went back to dope.

Changed Lives

Soon after, a business offer came my way. One of my friend's brothers had his own business putting body side moldings on cars. It was a profitable business as he had connections with car dealers and body shops all around Massachusetts and Rhode Island. So I left the machine shop and went to work for him. While my buddy had a great thing going, he also had a problem. He was a degenerate gambler. When the bookies came after him, I wound up owning the business. I didn't know a thing about operating a small "legal" business, but that didn't matter. His accountant took care of the books, handling all tax issues. So suddenly I had some legitimate cash coming in. With an adjustment here and there, and with three guys working for me, I was doing okay.

But by now, my old friend, heroin, was back. My wife was no fool and she knew the signs when she saw them. She begged, she threatened, but it was no use. One day, we were supposed to go to my niece's first holy communion, but when my wife came home from work, she found me unconscious in the bathtub with a needle sticking out of my arm. That was it for her, she left that day and I never heard from her until I got the divorce papers in the mail. Several months later the divorce was final. I was really off and running!

Bankrupt
At least being married had given me some stability.

But with my wife gone, there was no longer a reason to keep up any kind of a front. My drug use went "through the roof," and I began blowing hundreds of dollars a day on dope. With that kind of habit, I needed cash badly. After my own money was gone, I started working the banks. I got dozens of credit cards and a few loans. Every time I sat at a bank manager's desk, signing my name to yet another set of papers, I had no plans of ever paying it back. Within a year's time, my credit was a disaster. I had burned everyone, and now they were screaming for their money.

One afternoon, I hauled two big shopping bags of bills into the office of a Boston lawyer that I was referred to by my friend's bookie. I had been out of jail for 11 years. I had tried to build a life for myself, but I lost it. As the lawyer watched, I dumped out the contents on his desk. There were dozens of bills from all my different creditors and I told him, "I owe these people over $80,000. Can you take care of this?"

The attorney seemed a little scared, so I gave him $300 in cash and left. A few weeks later in court, when a federal judge discharged me of all debt, I thought I had died and gone to heaven. Examining the papers he said simply, "I hereby declare you bankrupt." And that was it. He had no idea just how true that statement was.

Hopeless

To this day I can still remember making that clear, conscious vow. I was all the way out there; chasing dope and committing crime to get it. Once while driving down the road, it hit me that I would never amount to anything and there was no hope at all for me, ever! I was totally convinced that I couldn't live without dope. Even with a wife and a legitimate business falling in my lap, I screwed it all up. From deep inside, I made a vow in my heart, to dedicate my life to the pursuit of crime and narcotics. The sooner someone puts a bullet in my head, the better. I was absolutely hopeless.

I ran into a friend of mine who had stolen some blank prescription pads but didn't know what to do with them. I knew how to write scripts and I hatched a plan. We began stealing prescription pads from hospitals and doctor's offices. We went to drugstores all over New England and even hired a few other people to partner with us. We would go to pharmacies and "cash" them. Then we would drive back to Boston with bottles and bottles of narcotics. I would sell the pills on the street for top dollar and use the money to buy heroin.

I was "in business" again. I kept an organized record of the town, the pharmacy, what drug I wrote the script for, how many pills, what name I used, which doctor's script and his DEA number. I was very careful; I did not want to go back to jail.

> My whole life was now centered on stealing scripts,
> cashing them and shooting dope.
> Every ounce of energy went to satisfy
> one thing - my craving for dope.

As I drove through New England, I would see young couples with their kids or walking with their arms around each other. It was like a different world, a world I knew I would never know. Once in a while, thoughts of my father would come to mind, but he was gone. I lost Ma to alcohol, lost a wife and any hope for a future. I truly believed that I was no good and never would be. Now I was just a stone-cold, "hope-to-die" dope fiend.

Maybe Someone's Trying To Tell Me Something

Right from the beginning I sensed something was wrong. I had just handed a script to the pharmacist in a drug store in the suburbs. He looked at the script, then he looked at me. Something in his eyes had changed. He hesitated. "I'm a little busy, so it'll be a few minutes," he said. "You can look around the store while I fill this for you." My antenna went up! "I've got another errand. I'll be back," I said casually, and went back to my car and drove a few blocks away. I found a pay phone and waited about twenty minutes. I called the pharmacy and asked if it was ready. There was a slight hesitation in the young woman's voice. Then she said "Uh, yeah. You can come get it now." When I pulled into the parking lot everything looked quiet, but I still parked close to the road. There was a kid getting out of a car beside me. I said "Hey, kid, come here." He came to the car window, and I held up a twenty. I told him "I just got my leg out of a cast and I can't walk too well. Here's twenty bucks if you'll go and get my medicine for me."

He was in the store less than two minutes, when I saw him come back to the front door with the store manager and two cops. He pointed out my car, and at the same moment, from behind the store, I saw several police cars come flying out. My foot slammed on the gas pedal, and I was gone.

Three police cars pulled in line behind me, as I ran red lights and jumped sidewalks, speeding out of town. I had only one thought as I drove like a madman: they're going to have to kill me because I'm not going back to jail. As I was driving, I began chewing and eating as many pills as I could. As I was being chased, I would pass from one town through another. Each time I went through a new town more police cars from that town joined in the chase. I had already gone through three towns and I could see the red-flashing lights of a dozen or more cruisers in my rearview mirror.

Suddenly, the cruiser behind me pulled out of the line and sped up until he was on my right side going the wrong way down the street. When I looked over at the cop, he rammed his car into mine. The jolt knocked me and my left tires dropped off the edge of the road. I held onto the steering wheel, jerked it to the right and got back onto the road. My foot never left the gas pedal.

The cruiser was still coming and I knew he would try to ram me again. But this time I was waiting for him. When I saw him coming up beside me again, I turned my wheel to the right and slammed hard into his driver side. The jolt, the sound of screeching metal on metal, was incredible. I slammed the cruiser off the road and into a ditch. In my mirror I could see the next car speed up, pulling up fast behind me. I thought, is this cop going to be stupid enough to try it too? Didn't he see what I just did to the other one? I came to an intersection, and to avoid hitting several cars and people, spun around in a circle. I was on sidewalks, going down one-way streets, doing everything I could to shake these guys. Then I came to the top of hill and the road turned sharply. I dropped my eyes from the rearview mirror, I spun the wheel, but it was too late. Dead ahead was a huge tree; there was nowhere to turn.

How I survived the crash I do not know. The police flung open the car door, dragged me out onto the ground and surrounded me. Dazed from the drugs and the crash, I looked up at revolvers and policemen who wanted to shoot me. At that moment, I wanted to die and I was praying that they would kill me. I was not lucky enough to get my wish. I guess God had other plans. The charges against me included dozens of narcotics violations, and also the attempted murder of a police officer with a motor vehicle. My business partner got ahold of my bondsmen and bailed me out.

> In the next three weeks, I got busted six times
> on new charges in six different counties.

I used up all my bondsmen because I kept getting arrested and never showed up to court. I couldn't stop the cycle; the whole world was caving in on me.

Something Seems To Be Happening

Although I was facing years in prison, it seemed like some kind of amazing grace was starting to intervene. I really needed help and there was a tiny, tiny part of me that thought it still might be possible to change. I didn't really believe it myself, but I was beginning to hope. I knew the State Hospital was no good, I hated it there. I heard that the Veteran's Administration had a drug addiction unit and I also knew that in the 70's they started using your social security number as your service ID. (One time when I was 19 years old and doing time, Ma came to see me and told me I got drafted. I told her "Great! Get them to open these doors and I'll be on my way". Naturally, it was a mistake. They must have forgotten that I was a junkie and they definitely didn't know I was doing time again). I went to the VA drug unit in Boston and told them I was a veteran and needed help. I was there for a few days, but it wasn't working. I finally admitted I wasn't really a veteran and they threatened to bring federal charges against me for falsifying my records. They were throwing me out, but they wouldn't let me leave without me calling someone to come pick me up. I didn't have a penny on me and all they had was a pay phone. The unit supervisor gave me one dime and told me if I can't get someone on this call, he was going to call the police and have me arrested. So I called Jack, my ex-brother-in-law, who was an old friend and a cop. He was on duty, but I told the dispatcher I was his brother and that it was an emergency. They connected me to him in his police car. He was just getting off duty and he came right away and took me home. I started looking for a program.

The only program that would take me was in Roxbury, MA called "The Third Nail." It was a last stop, hardcore, "therapeutic community" for junkies. Their method was to break you down and then build you back up in a positive way. They took away everything and shaved your head. They wanted to get past all your defenses. Then their counselors could rebuild you. I knew the routine, and so it didn't have too much effect on me. Besides, I was long past caring about anything. Inside I knew I was going to be a hopeless dope fiend all my life.

They had a court liaison on staff. When he did my first

interview, I thought he was going to have a nervous break-down. Over that past month, I had amassed over 200 charges in five different courts.That's why it seemed like a true mira-cle when each judge I went before was "somehow moved" to allow me to go through the program in spite of my exten-sive criminal background. My lawyer, the liaison and I were stunned. However, the judges told me that if this didn't work, I would probably be spending the rest of my life in prison as a habitual offender.

One day, some news reporters came to the program and asked the director if he had any "cases" they could use in a NBC-TV documentary. The program was co-ed, so they wanted one guy and one girl. The director said, "I got some-one." My life was such a mess due to drugs, I fit the bill per-fectly. The documentary wanted to illustrate how drugs mess up lives and it was narrated by Dan Travanti of Hill Street Blues. I called Ma and told her I was going to be on TV and she said, "What did you do now?" I thought, what a sad way to memorialize your life.

In Comes Jesus

I didn't know it at the time, but the summer before, Da-vid Wilkerson had come to Boston to do some street meet-ings. He didn't know his way around the bad spots, so he asked a former addict from Roxbury to take him around the housing projects and neighborhoods. After all the street meetings were over, the former addict, his wife and their children started ministering at local jails and drug programs. Then one night they came to "The Third Nail." The director asked if anyone wanted to go to church. I figured I might get out of the building for a while, so I said "yes." Instead of going out, they took me and a few other guys up to the third floor. I was a little confused.

There was a big guy, Pete, his wife and six kids. As I sat in my chair to hear him talk, I was surprised to see the black book he was holding in his hand. It looked like a Bible. I had never seen one up close, only in the movies, but I was curious. No one had ever, in my whole life, talked to me from the Bible. He looked at me and told me something I had never heard. "Jesus loves you and He knows what you've been going through. He knows everything you ever did, and He still loves you. Not only that, but He wants to help you and give you a new life." After years of listening to every crook, junkie and deviant on the streets and in jail, his words seemed to ring true and honest. They were more real than anything I had ever heard.

I hadn't set foot in a church in almost twenty years, but in the back of my head, I did believe in God. I guess I believed in Jesus Christ too, but it never occurred to me that if Jesus was God, then He was alive today. "He knows all about what's been going on in your life," Pete went on. "And He cares about you." God cares about me? I'd never heard this kind of talk before. It sounded strange because I didn't even care about myself, how could God?

But something in his words shot deep into my heart. He continued, "God knows all about your lying, stealing, every bad thing you ever did and He still cares about you. That's why He died, to pay the price for your sins." Then he asked me if I wanted to say a prayer with him and ask Jesus to forgive me for all the bad things I ever did and to start a new life with Jesus. So I did. After that, his wife and kids sang a couple of Christian songs. From my Catholic background, this was also a new experience.

Each Friday, Pete came back to talk to us from the Bible. He was the only real Christian I had ever met in my whole life. Everything he said was like a message that was becoming clearer and clearer. Everything I had ever tried failed but just maybe, there was something to Jesus. Maybe someone was trying to tell me something. For the first time in my life since my father died, I opened up to the possibility that maybe someone cared about me after all.

Slow Change

Previously, I had heard about people "turning their life over to God" and usually, it sounded like they went from being John Dillinger to an apostle overnight. That definitely was not the case for me. After a couple of months, the director stopped Pete from coming to preach at the program because too many guys were attending. They said it was interfering with our "treatment." So my discipleship was put on the back burner. With six court stipulations and years hanging over my head, I had to finish the program. When I was in the last phase of the program, they referred me to the Fernald State School to apply for a job as a direct care worker with the developmentally disabled as part of my exit plan.

I finished the program in 1982, but my interest in Jesus had dwindled. Still, I was determined not to shoot dope or drink. At the Fernald School out of thirty five buildings the only opening on their grounds was in the lone "locked building." That meant that every door you went through in the entire building had to be opened with a key and then locked behind you. The guys on this ward were in their twenties and thirties and seriously developmentally disabled. They were extremely violent and self-abusive. In my unit there were only six clients with three of us staff on duty at all times. Though the conditions were rough, I loved it and I loved them. When I was being hired, the woman knew I was coming out of a program and she said that guys with my background usually worked pretty well with these hard cases, she was right.

Immediately, I found I could work with these guys. I seemed to be able to connect with them because they were like me in a way. They were largely forgotten and discarded. No one came to see them or even cared they existed except some of us who worked with them daily. I found myself becoming attached to these guys. As the months passed, I found myself looking forward to seeing them every morning and even looking forward to going to work! Maybe it was this was the first time I felt like I belonged and was doing something worthwhile.

But I still wasn't concerned with "religion." I was trying to catch up with some living that I had missed growing up. I wasn't drinking, shooting dope or doing crime, but I still thought, "Everybody has to have something." I still was thoroughly convinced that I couldn't go through life without being high. So I began to smoke pot. Then I figured I would sell just a little to a few people I worked with so I wouldn't have to pay for my own.

So now I spent my time working, smoking pot, dealing a little, and going out with some of the girls at work. I had an old car and I rented a room from a girl I knew. Within a year, I got a raise and I was in line to become a supervisor of one of the buildings. I was doing so well with these difficult guys that they wanted to pay for me to go to college and become better trained. Even Ma thought I had finally made it. But by the end of 1983, something kept bothering me. I knew that just smoking pot wasn't going to last. I threw a punch at one of the guys at work one day, and I knew I was beginning to lose my grip. I knew that eventually I would be back on dope if I kept going down this path. I kept thinking back to that time I had asked God to help me and it really began to haunt me. Every night I stared at the Good News Bible on the nightstand that Pete had given me, but I never read it. Things were starting to get very uncomfortable and I thought that this might finally be the end of me.

A Thunderbolt From Heaven

It was Thursday night, January 19, 1984. I was all alone in my apartment when it (He) hit me. I fell down on my knees beside the bed and I can still remember the words that came out from deep inside.

> "I'm done, God!" I prayed. "I'm done fighting you.
> I don't know what you want with me,
> or what you want to do with me."

"I don't know if you want me to become a priest and wear a robe or what. But, whatever it is, I'm giving you my life—all of it—to do whatever you want with it."

Suddenly, I felt something powerful come over me. I was filled with boldness and my fear was gone. I could sense God's words passing right through me saying, "Don't worry, kid, everything is going to be all right. Don't be afraid. I'm going to give you a whole new life."

I got up off my knees a different person. I grabbed my stash of weed and immediately flushed it down the toilet. It was incredible. I was like a madman, but in a good way. I ran across the hall to the girl I was renting from, and started telling her I was going to be a Christian. She thought I was crazy. At work, I started blurting out to everyone, "Guess what! I'm going to be a Christian." I still really had no idea what this meant. Mainly, the people at work looked at me like I was losing it and if I were in their shoes I would have, too.

Then I called the only Christian I knew in the whole world, Pete, the guy who came to minister to me at The Third Nail. I hadn't talked to him in three years. I said, "Pete, I want you to make me a Christian. I want you to teach me all about Jesus. Can I move in with you guys?" Thank God that Pete was as crazy as I was. He said yes, and told me I could come and live with him and his family in Roxbury. So I quit my job, which I loved, left my friends and moved in with Pete. I gave him all the money I had and told him, "OK, here's all I got, now you own me, but you have got to feed me". His wife and kids took me in like a lost brother. They were poor as church mice, but soaked in humility and kindness. Pete was driving a van for the Salvation Army at the time. He spent all his time talking to people about God and telling them about Jesus. If ever

I needed evidence that God cared for His own, it came to me through Pete and his family. Their kindness and generosity, not to mention the intensity of their faith, was like nothing I had ever experienced in my life. I read my entire Bible, cover to cover, in six months. I really wanted to learn about Jesus.

Then a very, very strange thing happened. It was Mother's Day and I hadn't told Ma about anything that that had happened yet. I had saved $500 for her before I gave the rest to Pete. So I called her up and asked her if she wanted me to come over and have some supper with her since it was Mother's Day. She said that it would be okay.

I bought a plant for her and went over. She made a steak for me, but she didn't have anything but her drink. I gave her the plant and the money and was thinking of what to say. As I was eating, I said, "Ma, I got something to tell you." She asked me if I was in trouble again and I said "No, not that."

"Well what is it?" she said.

"I quit my job and I'm going to be a Christian."

"What?" she said.

"I gave my life to Jesus Christ."

As soon as I said Jesus Christ, she threw her arm up in the air and her eyes started to water up. She just stared at me. I said, "What's the matter Ma, are you okay?" I thought she was having a heart attack or something. She said, "Your father made me promise never to tell you."

"Tell me what?" I said.

"You're not our kid."

"What do you mean I'm not your kid?"

"You're not our kid."

"Well whose kid am I?"

"I don't know", she said. "We got you out of the Harley Hospital in Dorchester, Massachusetts."

It felt like the life was draining out of me as I sat there trying to eat my steak and be cool. My "roots" were ripped out in one conversation. Everything I had ever thought about, who I was and where I came from, were gone. By now, she was crying and I could see that she was very upset. I didn't want to hurt her anymore so all I could think of to say was, "Don't worry about it, Ma. As far as I'm concerned you are my mother." My attempted consolation didn't seem to help she was still very upset. She told me that they were unable to have kids due to my father's condition after the war. Since they wanted to have a family, so they looked into adoption. She said that he brought me home from the hospital one day, but they were never allowed to know who the real parents were. The laws were very strict about concealing the identity of biological parents in those days. I finished my supper and tried to calm her down as best I could, and then I left.

Driving back to Roxbury was surreal. Thank God it was in His timing that I found out about my adoption now and not

132

when I was younger. I don't know how my immature self would have handled it. Still, my head was spinning. I kept asking myself, "Did I just hear what I think I heard?" It was absolutely bizarre. When I pulled up to Pete's house he was standing on the sidewalk talking to someone. I guess I looked a little rattled because as soon as he saw me he said, "What happened to you?" I told him the whole story and he was as dumbfounded as I was, but my new family helped me understand that God was still, and always, in control.

Teen Challenge

One day, I said to Pete, "You know, it's too bad they don't have drug programs like the one I was in, only Christian."

He said, "Someone does have programs like that."

"You're kidding?" I said.

"Yeah," he said. "A pastor named David Wilkerson started those years ago."

"Boy would I like to see them," I said. Because Pete and his family "lived by faith" he said he knew David Wilkerson and some other people in Teen Challenge centers, and he would take me to see them.

We prayed and trusted God for our new mission to pursue. Pete gave up his apartment in Roxbury, we paid all the rent money, and then me, Pete, his wife and six children, including a newborn baby, all loaded into my car and started heading south. Pete's plan was to take me to Teen Challenge centers all down the east coast. "We will trust God to direct us," he said. "We'll go to every Teen Challenge center that will let us in and ask them if they will put us up for a couple of days while we minister to the guys. I will bring the message, my wife and kids will sing and you can tell how God has freed you from a whole lifetime of drug addiction." With the same enthusiasm I threw into pursuing dope, I now began to pursue a new life.

What followed was nothing less than six months of small but definitive miracles. God opened doors for us to stay at nearly every Teen Challenge center from Brooklyn to Georgia.

> We would do chapels and services,
> ministering to the guys about the freedom from
> drug addiction though Jesus Christ.

Always, our talks were followed by an invitation to a meal, a place to spend a night or two, or to speak at a local church. I was getting a hands-on education of living by faith and how God answers prayers. I began to really believe that God was taking care of us.

As all this was going on, I started to realize that I had another Father standing in the wings, ready to look out for me and help me through life. Now, through every little miracle of help and provision I was witnessing on this trip, every message and reading my Bible, it seemed God was saying to me, "Let me be your Father, and you won't ever have to feel like you're on your own again. I'll take care of all the anxieties you used to have when you believed you were totally alone in the world. I am giving you a new life."

As we headed back to Boston, I wondered what I was going to do when we got there. We had no place to stay, but the string of events that followed, like some kind of divine clockwork, was remarkable. Pete introduced me to Rodney Hart who was in the process of starting a Teen Challenge program in Boston. Rodney didn't have any openings for me at the time, but after speaking with me he called the Teen Challenge center in Brockton and I was hired.

In the thirty years since I began working with Teen Challenge, I can tell you that my life has not been all that easy, but it has most definitely been blessed! I've been blessed with personal miracles—such as Shirley, my wife, life partner, and best friend. Unfortunately, I lost Shirley to cancer in 2006, but I continue to thank God for allowing her to be part of my life for 14 years. I miss her greatly, but I know she is with the Lord, and I am looking forward to the day when I will go to be with Him, and see her again.

I have also been blessed with daily miracles at work, like seeing funds come in at times when needs in the program are critical and by seeing all the other Teen Challenge lives that are changed miraculously, right before my eyes.

Most of all, I've been blessed every day of my life knowing that I was once a kid who lost his father, and then lost his way. I grew to be a man who believed that no one cared about me, so why should I care about myself? I was once alone and destined to a life of failure. Today, I know that I have a God and Father Who will always take care of me and never leave me. For me, and many others that I have met through my Christian life, Jesus miraculously stepped in when we were utterly lost and without any hope. He gave me a new heart and a new life, and I will never forget that. This is our message to everyone who comes to Teen Challenge. If He could change our lives, He can change yours!

Chapter 8
From Pride To Precious

Robyn Frye

I was born into a family of trail blazers. My family ha
a rich cultural history and a sense of pride. Being half West
Indian and half from the Deep South, these characteristics
should have been ingrained in me. But being raised during the
social upheaval of the Civil Rights Movement, should it really
have been a surprise that it was my differences that shaped
my early life?

I received tall genes from my parents. My father was
6 feet 8 inches tall and my mother was 5 feet 11 inches tall.
When I was a newborn, everyone present in the hospital room
couldn't believe how long I was. This was the beginning of my
life of coping with being different, mainly taller, than everyone
else. There were standing jokes about by size from the very
beginning, even before I entered into kindergarten. My family
and cousins would joke and say things like, "She looks like

Olive Oyl from the cartoon "Popeye" and "Her feet are big enough to be snow skis." While I laughed along on the outside, I was always deeply hurt on the inside. My family was made up of proud people, so I was not allowed to let anyone know how hurt I truly was. I laughed along as though nothing was bothering me, but inside I cried everyday.

My trail tlazer family had great expectations of me. My grandfather was a high-ranking Union leader that was even invited to President Jimmy Carter's inaugural ball. My father was one of the first African American FBI agents in the United States. My mother was one of the first black female models to go to print in the United States. Naturally, I was expected to also do something great and blaze a trail of my own.

When I was eight years old, my mother died a tragic death. I had no idea how to cope with the pain and sadness at that early age. So I did what I had always done; I hid the pain of my losing my mother inside. At the time, I was close to my aunt who acted as my caretaker when my mother traveled for work. My parents had been separated for several years. Once my mother passed, my aunt then took care of me as my guardian and I felt safe with her. As I continued to grow, I became a little girl in a woman's body. When I graduated junior high school at thirteen years old I was already 6 feet tall! I wanted to be accepted. I wanted to fit in. I wanted to be liked. I wanted to be loved. I wanted to be great at something. So

I did whatever it took to be accepted, to fit in and to be liked.

> The price I paid for acceptance was my
> introduction to drugs, alcohol and sex.

I can remember the first time I ever used a drug. I smoked marijuana and not long after the first few puffs, I couldn't see! It scared me at first but soon I found it helped me hide all of my feelings, my pain, as well as my fears. As time went by, I continued using marijuana daily in high school and I drank on the weekends. By the time I was a senior in high school I was using multiple types of drugs. In my sophomore year of high school, my addictions were already so strong that I was failing in all of my classes. I remember coming home high and telling my aunt I had to go to summer school because I had failed two classes. I remember feeling so stupid, so low and so bad about myself, that I just wanted it all to end.

When my aunt when to work that night, I took every prescription pill in the house and went to sleep. I woke up and realized I couldn't walk, everything in the room was moving all around me. I realized I would die if I didn't get help. I made it to the phone and I called another aunt. She was able to help me. As a result of that near-overdose, that summer I battled with migraines, dizziness, nausea and vomiting all while attending summer school. I never told anyone outside of my family what

I had done. I still had our family's pride ingrained in me, and I could never let anyone see my weakness. The following school year, I curbed my drug use and did better academically, eventually I graduated with honors.

The summer before my senior year, my grandmother passed away and my father, whom I had never really known, started coming to visit. I had no real interest in establishing a relationship with him, or any other man, at that point. Over the past few years, I had been hurt physically, sexually and emotionally by men. I just wanted to live for myself and do what I did best, making everyone believe I was all right.

It's hard to describe how horrible my life was. I was always feeling one way and having to hide those feelings and act a different way. But I did it because it was my coping mechanism. I have no idea how I made it to college, but I did. My freshman year I lived off-campus in my grandparent's house, with my grandfather. Eventually, he moved out to be closer to his work, and for the first time in my life I was on my own. Unfortunately, I hated every moment of my new living situation because I felt so alone.

I found myself at the top of a downward spiral of addiction, and I continued down this path for 16 years. All of the things I said I would "never" do, I did. I began running away from place to place, trying to escape my guilt and shame; I was far from being a "trail blazer." Then one day I just couldn't run any more, all I wanted was a chance to start over and have a "Changed Life!"

I entered in a program in 1992 called New Life for Girls, in Westminster, Maryland. The first Bible scripture they read to me was 2 Corinthians 5:17, "Therefore if any man (woman) be in Christ, he (she) is a NEW creature, old things are passed away. Behold ALL things become new." I remember thinking to myself, "What?! I could be NEW?!" All the other programs I had attempted to seek help from had told me I had an incurable disease; once an addict, always an addict. Well, 23 years later I am here to tell you that I was able to be made new, and that God is real and Jesus saves completely!

I wasn't perfect, but I was no longer the girl that I kept trying to run away from. After graduating the program and going through a divorce, God provided a sanctuary and a place of continued healing for me at the Restoration Home for Women in Providence, Rhode Island (Providence Teen Challenge Women's Home). It was there I received the deep healing in my soul which was necessary to prepare me for the wonderful man God had in store for me. I met my husband Everette when he was the house supervisor for the Boston and Providence Teen Challenge Men's Homes. God molded us and shaped us to serve together, and we've now been married for 15 years! After working side by side in ministry for two years we were called into the marketplace to be "salt" in the world and gain experience in living for Christ outside of the ministry.

After moving on from the Restoration Home for Women, I served in a professional capacity supporting neighborhood resident groups and non-profit organizations by facilitating meetings, forums and community change models. I have been honored by Senators and Congressmen for my community work and appointed by Mayors. I received many awards and honors, but at the end of the day, ALL glory and honor goes to God alone!

Today, I am a Before and After Site Director. God has given me a passion for both youth empowerment and social change. My educational background includes: majoring in Elementary Education at Adelphi University in Garden City, New York, and later I received my certification in Social Entrepreneurship from the Massachusetts Institute of Technology (MIT).

> God had opened many doors for me to make a difference in people's lives and to be a trail blazer!

I was selected to Co-Chair the United Way of RI Community School Initiative in Providence, Rhode Island. I was appointed by former Mayor David N. Cicillini, a member of the Providence Public School Board and the Eli Broad Institute for School Boards, where I was conferred the title of Broad Fellow. I have had the privilege of serving as volunteer support and chaplain in several correctional faculties throughout the country including Maryland, Chicago and Rhode Island. Now God has called my husband Everette and me into birthing a men's long-term residential substance abuse ministry. We believe and trust God for everything because God has always been so faithful.

The good news is what Teen Challenge and the Lord has done for me He will do for anyone who comes to Him and believes that He has the power to create "Changed Lives."

There's a song that says, "There's no way I'll ever doubt Him... I know too much about Him... Jesus is REAL to me."

Chapter 9
Homeless & High

Paul Gifford

The following is a chronicle of a series of critical events in my life that helped shape me to become a man after God's own heart. My life has been radically changed by the power of God and I live to tell my story of His saving grace, mercy and love.

Try it Once

I have news for whoever said; "Just one time won't hurt you" because they were very WRONG. That one time set the wheels in motion for my journey through drug and alcohol addiction, a journey that lasted for almost twelve years.

Former One Times:

One time I had no father - that lasted for 18 years
One time I carried a gun - that lasted for 7 years

Changed Lives

One time I smoked a cigarette - that lasted for 12 years
One time I smoked marijuana - that lasted for 10 years
One time I drank alcohol - that lasted for 10 years
One time I had sex outside of marriage - that lasted for 8 years
One time I snorted cocaine - that lasted for 8 years
One time I smoked crack - that lasted for 2 years
One time I used ecstasy - that lasted for 8 years
One time I slept on the street - that lasted for 2 years
One time I ate thrown out KFC - that lasted for 2 years
One time I overdosed - and that was it.

Latter One Times:

One time I met my heavenly father - that has lasted
for 13 years
One time I read the entire Bible - that has happened 13 times
One time I graduated college - that happened in 2006
One time I met my wife – to whom I've been happily and faith-
fully married for 11 years
One time I brought a son into the world - that happened
3 times
One time I received a call to ministry – I have been a pastor
for 7 years
One time I coached a sport - that has lasted for 4 years
One time I helped to write a book and this is my
'Changed Life' story

Biography

I was born on May 15, 1976 in Brooklyn, New York, one of two children. My mother was a hard-working, 23 year old, college student and employee. In early 1978 we moved to the outskirts of Boston, Massachusetts where I spent the next twelve years of my childhood. Although our home life looked like we had it all together, it was actually unraveling. My father was not motivated to provide for our family and this brought tremendous strain on my parents' relationship. Soon they arrived at the awful place of divorce.

Since my father was not around during the most crucial times of my life, I do not have fond memories of him. As a child, I remember staring out the front window on specific birthdays and holidays, while waiting for the knock on the door that never happened.

The Battle Begins

While mom worked two jobs, she finished her education and raised two kids in a rough neighborhood. At a young age, I had to take on responsibilities that I probably shouldn't have had to. I was the one who had to make sure my little sister was fed, got on and off the bus for school, and in bed on time.

Changed Lives

> Crime was on the rise in my neighborhood and
> at the age of eleven I witnessed
> two murders right before my eyes.

Drugs were everywhere around me, I was chased by armed gang members, and I was sexually molested by a babysitter.

One day I thought that it would be a great idea for me to swipe a cigarette from my mother's pack of Salem Lights. I ran down to the corner of my best friend's apartment and together we took a journey into the golf course not too far from my house. As he lit the match and I watched the end of the cigarette glow I couldn't believe it was about to hit my lips and rush into my lungs. That was my first head rush and at the time it was the most exhilarating experience I'd ever had. For the next two minutes everything began to spin out of control and then I suddenly felt calm. I couldn't wait to get my hands on the next cigarette.

Most of what I learned came from the streets. As the saying goes, "If you can't beat 'em, join 'em." I began to carry a 9mm handgun all throughout high school which gave me a great sense of protection and safety. I was truly a city kid with a city mentality.

My best friend, who I smoked that first cigarette with, was shot and killed during a raid that went terribly wrong in his project apartment. The news of his murder devastated me, yet in the back of my mind, I was thankful I was not in the apartment with him that day. We were known to be inseparable. By 1989, my mother knew that we couldn't survive any longer living on the outskirts of Boston. We were poor and the economic outlook for the area was bad. We moved 27 miles south of Boston to the town of Bridgewater, Massachusetts. I knew she made the right decision.

In the city, I had been the minority, all my friends were African American or Spanish, but now everyone was Caucasian. This felt a bit strange, because they acted and dressed so differently from what I was used to.

Anger and frustration began to grow inside of me and having no father in my life didn't help matters. One afternoon in the 8th grade, I just couldn't take any more of the constant bullying from this one kid in class. I had asked him four times to stop flicking me in the ear with his pencil. Finally, I reacted by sucker punching him and he went down for the count with a broken jaw in three places. Suddenly this city kid commanded some respect in his new town.

After school one day, some new friends and I went down a road where I met something that would minimize all the difficult emotions I was struggling with. I clearly remember one friend said; "Wait here, I will be right out. I have something to get inside my house." When he came out we went to a school playground where he asked, "Have you ever smoked one of these?" I said, "A cigarette?" He said, "No, weed." I told him I hadn't, but I wouldn't mind trying something new. He said, "You'll never be the same again." As we sat inhaling and exhaling the joint, I realized things suddenly became a little bit more interesting than when smoking just a regular cigarette. I was now "high" for the first time in my life and he was right, I was never the same after that day. Every weekend we got together to smoke weed and get high.

My world had completely changed! I loved all the high school extracurricular activities; sports, parties and friends. I had learned on the street to do anything for anybody. I would have put my life on the line for any one of my friends and I had their back. Little did they know that it included a "packed" belt buckle. What started out as a sense of protection from the city life, transitioned to thinking that I was protecting "my boys" and "my girls."

Cottonmouth was the term we used when your tongue would stick to the roof of your mouth from doing drugs. Once water or Coca-Cola wasn't doing the trick anymore, while a freshman in high school, I was introduced to "Mr. Whiskey and Coke." Three twelve-ounce drinks later, I was drunk for the first time in my life. That year we would hit my friend's parents' liquor cabinet on Friday nights. This set the stage for the rest of my high school social drinking experience, which was done at pit parties, house parties, bars and clubs.

Partying was the norm for me by 1994. Since this was my graduation year, I was on a mission to make sure I didn't miss one opportunity to live it up. What began as a weekend social habit, had became a daily necessity. I was going to class high, driving high and/or drunk, playing sports high, and working high. I had moved on from weed; cocaine, ecstasy, acid, club drugs and alcohol had taken over. After learning that my basketball dream was over due to a severe knee injury, I went into a deep, dark place inside. Basketball had been the only thing keeping me somewhat motivated in life. Outwardly, I did a pretty good job making sure nobody knew that my personal life was out of control, or at least I thought so.

> Many times after passing out I would wake in some places that would baffle the human mind. One night it was a snow bank, another night it was my front lawn, and once it was in a jail cell.

The most embarrassing and yet horrifying place, was when my mother found me in my bedroom closet, naked, with my eyes rolled back in my head. The reality hit my mom that her son was in big trouble. I am certain that she knew I was doing some teenage things, but not to this extent. Just a few days later my mom went away and I had the opportunity to throw a house party. I never imagined that the house party would grow to the size of over 300 people. By 1:30 am it was out of control. I heard sirens and half of the Bridgewater Police Department was chasing kids through my living room and back yard. Some managed to escape on foot, but most were forced to surrender their licenses to the officers. We were given specific instructions by the police that we had 36 hours to show up downtown with our parents or we would lose our licenses and pay a fine. The story was so big it hit the front page of the local newspaper.

The very next day my mom had reached her breaking point. She decided that it would be best if I wanted to continue living this type of lifestyle that I would have to "get out of her house." I had never been confronted with a decision like that before, but being the knuckle-headed kid that I was, I choose to leave the house and move in with a friend.

I managed to graduate high school and get a job working in a warehouse making pretty decent money. From this day forward, work was never a problem for me. I worked several jobs making good money while maintaining my expensive drug addiction. Life at 18 years old was pretty good! I had money, sex, drugs, a brand new SUV, and lots of entertainment. On top of all that, to make a little extra money on the side, I started selling cocaine.

There were moments over the next couple of years that I thought about going to college, but it wasn't until the summer of 1997 after I moved to Fitchburg, Massachusetts that I began to take classes at Fitchburg State University. I wasn't much of a campus person, but through a few college parties, I met some guys who were renting a house on Highland Avenue. It was known as one of the roughest areas in the community, but having grown up in the city, it was like home for me. I moved into a fraternity house and over the next two years my life spiraled down, right to hell.

I lost touch with reality and family members, including my mother and sister. I couldn't figure out what I wanted to do, where I wanted to go or who I wanted to be. For the first time in my life, I was hit with a great sense of loss and confusion. I had no father, no mother, no sister, no real friends, a girlfriend of two years left me, work wasn't satisfying. I dropped out of college for the third time and my life pretty much sucked. I found myself blaming everybody but me, which is exactly what addicts do. It's always everybody else's fault. I tried to claw my way out, but couldn't. So I just stayed where I was hiding - in bars or clubs, drunk and high.

By 1999, I packed up and landed at my aunt's house in Cranston, Rhode Island. For the first time finding and keeping a job was very difficult because of my addiction. I soon explored cooking cocaine on a spoon which led to smoking crack cocaine. As if I needed to get hooked on another kind of drug! But oh my, talk about being with your own thoughts and having not a care in the world!

> I thought crack cocaine was one of my best friends.
> Before long it brought me to a place of utter darkness
> and despair. Once hooked, I found myself homeless.

For two years I lived between Providence, Rhode Island and Boston, Massachusetts; under bridges, in subway stations, bus terminals, dark alleyways and in bars. I was standing on my last leg as I fought to remain high enough to survive to see the next day. Outside of robbing people, I would do anything to make money, including selling drugs. I figured this is how I will spend the rest of my life or I will die trying.

On February 12, 2001, time, as I knew it, stopped. After making a run to Providence, I was inside a familiar vacant warehouse to celebrate. I opened up my eight ball and began snapping lines; I drank three 40 oz bottles of malt liquor and swallowed a few pills. The next morning, I was found just outside the Providence Bus Terminal unresponsive. Paramedics revived me inside the ambulance on the way to the hospital. That day I cried out for help knowing that I wouldn't live much longer if things didn't drastically change. At 24 years old, I believe God's hand came down and took hold of me to give me a "Changed Life."

I was released from the hospital at 7:05 a.m. and started my journey walking on Highway 95 north towards Boston. I managed to walk past two exits and as I looked up a hill the sun was beaming on a pay phone. I reached in my pocket and pulled out the calling card I had carried with me. It didn't have much time left on it, but I began dialing the numbers I had with me. The first call there was no answer, the second call no answer, and the third call no answer. The fourth call was to my father. Finally, my father had picked up the phone. I said; "Yo, Pop. I'm in a big mess and I need help, can I come and stay with you?" His response was, "No you can't stay with me, but I can pick you up and bring you somewhere."

Twenty-five minutes later he pulled up to the Shell gas station in his green Nissan Frontier. For the next thirty five minutes we didn't say a word to each other. He pulled around the bend of a driveway and down towards a steel structured building. The awning that covered the entrance to the building read "Teen Challenge New England" I thought to myself, "Does this guy even know how old I am?" The first words out of my mouth were "Seriously, this is where you are bringing me?" He said, "Trust me." I grabbed my plastic bag, which had one change of clothes; hauled my 105 pound weary body out of the car and headed into the facility as my father drove away.

I headed to the welcome desk and I said, "Hi, I'm here to check myself in." The secretary called for the intake pastor and I was told to go on ahead up the stairwell. I entered the pastor's office and spent the next several minutes explaining my addiction to drugs and alcohol. I was then handed a 15-page packet of Teen Challenge guidelines, I read the first two pages, laughed and threw the packet on the desk and headed for the exit. I got to the top of the driveway and was met by two men. The two guys turned me around walked me back towards the lobby and said, "Give it one day."

The next eight days were the most terrifying days of my life as I detoxed on a bottom bunk in a dorm room with four other guys. My physical body was going through withdrawals, cold sweats, fever, vomiting, shakes, and headaches. I thought to myself, "Today might just be the day that I die." But I guess God had other plans because I made it through!

Sunday evening February 19, 2001 is a day I will never forget. It was the first time I had stepped foot inside a church since 1993. My mother had done a great job making sure her children were brought up around Christian principles, but the choices I made led me away from a relationship with Jesus Christ. I knew about God, I could even quote a few scriptures, but I had no desire to live my life following Jesus. I was a prodigal son! However, this Sunday evening was the church service that God had set up specifically for me. As the preacher closed the service, he stepped down off the platform and sat down right next to me on the front row. He put his arm around me and uttered these words; "Son, you've tried a lot of things in your life to try to fill the void in your heart, can I ask you to give Jesus one try?" Without hesitation, I shook my head in a motion with my chin up and chin down, my head between the palms of my hand and tears rolling down my face. He said, "I promise He will not fail you, if you choose to put your trust in Him this night, the rest is history!"

The journey through the greatest drug and alcohol recovery program, Teen Challenge, would be the very place that God would set things in motion for the rest of my life. It was there that I learned how to love others. It was there I learned how to trust. It was there I learned obedience. It was there I learned sacrifice. It was there I learned humility. It was there I experienced the power of prayer when my mother was completely healed of breast cancer. It was through this answer to prayer that an entire house was radically changed. Since that answer to prayer, 17 of the 18 men that were in the house went into full time ministry serving the Lord. It was during this time that my mom and I would reconcile a broken relationship. It was there that I got a passion for God's Word. It was there where I got direction, and it was there where my life was changed. I completed the 15 month program! I was so indebted to those that made this possible and I knew God wasn't done with me yet. God wanted to use me to solidify my leadership skills and use me to help others that would come through the doors of Teen Challenge.

I remained on staff at Teen Challenge for 8 months working in the program development office. I was at a critical point in my journey and knew that God was taking me deeper in my studies. In January 2003, I began my pursuit of a bachelor's degree in Pastoral Ministries at Zion Bible College (now North Point). I had attempted college several times before but this time it was different because I had something to go after and I knew that God had a plan for my life.

My official four-year college stint became a fast track, which was accomplished in three years. I was passionate about my pursuit of Jesus, who remains the love of my life. Not only did I have my life calling, but my best friend Deena became my wife and life partner. It was 11 months after our first date on Valentine's Day 2003 that we joined our hearts and lives together on January 3, 2004 at the altar of a church in Toms River, New Jersey.

One of the greatest joys I share with my wife is how we remained sexually pure in our relationship until we had our first kiss at the altar during our wedding ceremony.

Although it was the most difficult thing I have ever had to abstain from, it did something for our relationship that was simply amazing!

Remember the father with whom I never had a relationship, the man who picked me up and brought me to Teen Challenge? Well the turning point in our relationship occurred one afternoon on my way to work. Shortly after I hung up the phone from a conversation with my father, the Holy Spirit spoke to my heart. It was in this car and at this moment that the Spirit of God said, "Son, you need to go to that bagel shop and make things right with your dad." I responded, "Me?" I thought that I had left this at the altar and truly forgiven him for all he did to my sister and me. "What could you want me to go to that bagel shop to do?" I felt again the impression from the Spirit of God as He uttered these words, "He needs to hear it from you." The conversation with God was done at this point, I picked up the phone, called my boss and said, "I have to take care of something relating to my dad, is it ok if I come in a little late?" Without hesitation my boss said, "Sure."

I walked into the bagel shop to where my father was sitting, grabbed two hot cups of coffee, sat down, peered across the table and said, "Dad, I want you to know that I forgive you for everything… I don't need an explanation as to why, just know that I forgive you." Our conversation was not long that afternoon, but immediately I felt the walls of separation break down and we embraced as father and son.

Three days later, I received a phone call from the Attleboro, Massachusetts Police Department stating that my father was missing. An all-points bulletin went out for his green

Nissan Frontier. Police eventually found his truck in a shopping plaza and my father was inside in a coma. Paramedics brought him to a local hospital where he remained in a coma for three months. He never fully recovered from a very aggressive stage of cirrhosis of the liver, hepatitis C and diabetes. During the months of April - August, Deena and I would make daily trips between Rhode Island and Massachusetts and on August 18, 2004, my father slipped into eternity.

There are several things that I take away from this time with my dad. I am eternally grateful for the opportunity to have had a relationship with him during the few months after he survived the coma. I am grateful for the opportunity for him to have heard my first sermon preached in his own home church. I am grateful that my first sermon preached at a funeral was his. I am grateful for the prophetic word he carried for his son, that he would live to see the day when I would live for the Lord and be married.

If this tragedy wasn't enough, within the next four months I would watch in hopelessly as Deena miscarried our first child, and as her family would say goodbye to her grandmother. I wasn't sure how I was going to get through all this, so I went to a familiar place, this time not drugs or alcohol; but my knees. I spent days in the Zion Chapel just waiting for a Word from the Lord. I want you to know that after pressing into prayer, God came through! One evening, the Spirit of

God assured me of this simple, but profound passage, "I will never leave you, or forsake you." That's all I needed. I had a renewed strength and determination to continue on.

I realize that if God is going to bring you into a storm, He will not leave you in that storm. The stormy seasons soon come to an end and we began to experience His blessings. I had the joy of seeing Deena receive her degree from Zion Bible College in May of 2005 and on September 23, 2005 we welcomed our first son into the world. I graduated Zion Bible College in May of 2006 and was licensed as a minister of the gospel of Jesus Christ with the Assemblies of God in June 2006. The next month, I followed the call of God to be the Associate Pastor of a church in Toms River, New Jersey. About a year later we welcomed our second son into the world on July 5, 2007.

God's blessings continued and a third son was born on July 31, 2009. In March of 2010, after a ten-month time of fasting and prayer, I followed the direction of the Lord and blessing of my district and sectional leaders to become the Lead Pastor of First Assembly of God in Toms River.

At the writing of this story, I have thoroughly enjoyed pastoring this growing church for the past four years. I have been faithfully married for ten years and together we are raising three amazing boys. From living on the city streets, eating out of garbage containers, intoxicating my body with all kinds of poison and having a near death experience, to have been given this day to live, is nothing short of a miracle! If it were not for God, I am sure I would not be breathing today.

If you are reading this story and have lost hope, let me share with you a scripture my mom first introduced to me, "For I know the plans I have for you declares the Lord, plans to prosper you and not to harm you, plans to give you a hope and a future." If you are struggling with addiction, or your marriage or have lost a child, hold on. If a parent has wounded you, forgiveness will make you both whole. Mom or Dad, if your child is using and abusing drugs, keep praying. Jesus will come to your rescue. God will be faithful to hear your heart's cry and do what He does best, "Change Lives."

Chapter 10
He Never Came Back

Oscar Cruz

I grew up in the small, Hispanic, farming town of Lamont, just on the outskirts of Bakersfield, California. Lamont is best known as a farming community and is located about an hour and a half north of Los Angeles. Families in Lamont were hardworking and many of the town's population were employed in the farming industry, working in the vineyards, potato fields and orchards.

My mother and father were both born in Mexico and came to the United States before I was born, so my first language is Spanish. I learned English when I began school. In Lamont, there was not much for kids to do, and I found myself going to school, coming home and playing in the yard or working with my family. I was the only boy in the family, outnumbered by three sisters. My mom and dad worked in the vineyards trying to make ends meet to support a family with four children to feed. Life as a child was ordinary. I was just a kid growing up in the farming community of Lamont.

Growing up with three sisters, I naturally gravitated toward my dad and my dad and I became really close. My mom furthered her education by studying real estate. She and my dad began buying rental properties and rehabbing homes. At a young age, my dad would take me to work with him on the construction site, to fix up homes and to help maintain our rental properties. I loved working with my dad. I enjoyed learning from him and he became my very best friend. Many times I would stay home from school so that I could go to the work site with my dad and learn what was being done. I always looked forward to getting up and working with him.

> I was 14 years old when my life changed forever.
> My best friend, my dad, walked out the door.

He had said it many times before; only this time it was different. I knew my parents had not been getting along, but as a little kid, I really didn't understand or believe this day would come.

That day, I watched my dad jump in his truck and peel out of the driveway. I ran after him chasing the truck, crying, begging, and pleading with him to stay.

But my best friend, my dad, never looked back. I was left alone in the driveway. I would wait at night, when headlights would flash through the window, and I would look out, thinking, hoping and wishing that it was my dad. As time went on, I realized that he was not coming back and that everything he had been telling me for years, about not getting along with my mother, had come to fruition. My best friend, my dad never returned.

After my father left, his words replayed like a tape player in my mind. I remember him saying time and time again that someday he was going to leave and that it was going to be my mother's fault. Two years prior to his departure, my dad had started sleeping in my room at night; he would sleep on the bed and I would sleep on the floor next to him. As a young boy, I didn't understand my father's words or the disagreements my parents had. As a result, after he left, I began to become resentful towards my mom who had only loved and cared for me.

After my dad left, my mom tried everything she could to be there, but the family was left in shambles. My dad had cleaned out my mom's bank account, collected the rental property income and had left my mom empty handed with the children. Still I hoped my dad would return someday. As a young boy there were many things I did not understand, and he had been my hero.

Soon my mother had to provide for three growing teenagers and a cousin we had taken in. This required her being gone from home and working long hours just to make ends meet and enable us to survive.

Little by little, the hurt and rejection of my dad leaving took over my life. I grew to become angry and resentful. I couldn't process all that had happened, why my dad was gone and why my mom had been left to support us children alone. My hurt changed to anger, and I bottled it all up inside. There wasn't anyone to talk to, I had no outlet. My heart had been broken, but I could never have found those words at the time.

I ran away from all the hurt feelings and started experimenting with marijuana. It felt good to numb the pain. I had been introduced to it by hanging out with my older cousins. I remember sneaking behind my house to a RV, where I would smoke it alone. Soon after that, I started introducing marijuana to my friends.

My drug use quickly progressed from marijuana to cocaine. I watched my cousins glorify cocaine and it rapidly caught my interest. One of my cousins had some cocaine, and I begged him to let me try it. After he let me try it, I was instantly hooked. It made me feel like I was in control.

Many nights I would go to sleep before my mom came home. There was no one around to know what I was doing, and I felt like I could get away with anything and everything. The drug use continued until the day I went looking for cocaine and the dealer said he only had "meth" (methanphetomine). I asked him what meth was and he told me it was better than the cocaine. From that day forward, meth began to take over my life. I quickly became out of control and ran away from home. I started living with friends and shortly thereafter dropped out of school. By the age of 16, I was a full blown addict and by 18 years of age I had a drug possession record and nothing more than a string of shattered dreams and relationships. Though I was constantly using, the drugs left me empty inside. I was living the expected life of the fatherless, and according to statistics I was not going to make it.

I don't know if I would have stood a chance at all if it had not been for my step dad Raul, who entered my mom's life during my addiction. Shortly after they met, my mom told him about me and asked him if he could help me. She had done everything she could. She bent over backwards trying time and time again to relate to me. She tried to understand, but because of my anger, I did not respond to her desperate attempts to help me.

Raul was a Teen Challenge graduate from the1980's whose life was transformed and he had never returned to addiction.

He shared his testimony with me and told me there was hope.

171

Changed Lives

He told me about Jesus, how I could change my life and that I didn't have to live this way anymore. This was my first glimpse of hope, but I was still not ready to change.

After several attempts at recovery, I found hope and support to get my life back on track at Teen Challenge. It was at Teen Challenge that God began His work in my life. I became involved with an inner-city ministry in Los Angeles, called the Los Angeles Dream Center where I began helping inner-city children in needy, crime-ridden neighborhoods. My life was turning around, and God had provided me a way out of a life of addiction. While at this ministry, I met my wife of 14 years, Allie, who was serving the homeless on the streets of Santa Monica with another ministry at the Dream Center. She was giving a shopping cart to a homeless person but it had a broken wheel. I offered to fix the wheel and from that day on, we became friends. Several short months later, we were married at the young age of 21. Once married, we served in missions to inner city children in Los Angeles neighborhoods. Life was happy, other than the growing pains and adjustments of being young and newly married.

After some time, I bought into the lie that I needed to provide more for my family, even though, looking back, God was already providing enough for us. We lived on a simple stipend of just a few hundred dollars a month, but I remember we were happy and had everything we needed. Those were some of the happiest days of my life, but I started thinking that the "American Dream" would make me happier than I was. Little did I know where that path was going to lead me.

After some time, we moved back to my hometown, where my mother and my step dad had developed a successful real estate and mortgage business. I started to chase the American Dream and was driven by the desire to be successful in real estate. The drive for financial success slowly engulfed me and caused me to forget what God had done in my life. Before I knew it, I found myself hanging out at familiar places with old friends who were still using and selling drugs. They had progressed far worse from where they were as teens. I was slowly drifting away from everything that mattered to me. One bad decision led to another. I went back to cocaine, alcohol, pot and then all the way back to my full blown meth addiction. I kept telling myself that I had everything under control. I started to lie to cover up for what I was doing. I was coming home at all hours of the night and living a life of shame. From the outsider's perspective, it looked like I had it all together. I had a house, a car, and a successful business, the American Dream. But on the inside, I was a functioning drug addict, wearing a suit and a tie. The truth was, my life was in shambles. I was addicted again, and my marriage was falling apart because of my drug use and my shameful decisions. I quickly found myself shutting out my young wife and family who were desperately trying to help me. During this time in my life, my beautiful daughter Kylie was born. She was a miracle in the midst of my addiction. God used her to grab my attention. I didn't want to hurt my wife or daughter anymore, but I did not know how to stop.

> I was trapped in my addiction and couldn't see a way out. I wish I could explain the way meth takes over a person's life because it takes away everything that matters.

For months my wife prayed for me and desperately tried to help me. She tried everything, from flushing drugs down the toilet to getting me out of the wrong places. But things continued to spiral down from bad to worse. I remember the day she said, "Oscar, either you go to Teen Challenge and finish the program or you are going to lose your family. I love you and don't want you to die." I didn't come home that night; drugs had taken over my life. The months following were foggy at best. I found myself losing everything I thought was going to make me happy. I was broke, alone, and addicted. I made attempts to get help, but was unsuccessful. I remember going to sleep with drugs in my hand, waking up, and then padding the blankets to see where I had left them the night before. I had come to believe that like some people needed insulin to survive, I needed drugs to survive.

Months went by and I remember going to court and hearing the judge say the divorce is final, only my signature was needed. I knew at that moment that I was forever going to lose my family if I signed that paper. Time had run out for me. Something inside me said, "If you lose your wife and daughter, that will be it." Knowing that I didn't want to lose my family for good, I refused to sign the paper. Well-meaning people told my wife to go on with her life and that I would never change.

But within a few short weeks, in my desperation, I cried out to God. I knew that I needed to change and I knew that I wanted to change. I was no longer being asked to change, but through the pain and desperation, God opened my eyes to show me how empty my life had become and that I was fighting so hard to keep all the wrong things.

I remember getting on my knees, and saying, "Okay God, I'm ready." On June 5, 2005, I knocked on my family's door and said, "I'm ready to change, will you help me?" Immediately, before I had a chance to change my mind, my wife bought for me a one way ticket to Teen Challenge in Brockton, Massachusetts.

On Sunday, June 6, 2005, I stepped off the plane in Boston and called Teen Challenge to let them know that I was here for the program and needed a ride. They wanted to know who gave permission for me to come to the program and asked me who I had talked to. At that moment, I realized that I had gotten on a plane from California to Boston without asking Teen Challenge if they would accept me. They came and picked me up from the airport and brought me to the center. At first, it was questionable if they would even accept me, because I had brought drugs with me to the program and gave them up only when asked during the initial search process. They asked me, "Why would you bring drugs to the program?" My response was, "I can't get off drugs on my own, not ever." I remember thinking that I would do whatever I had to do to change. If they told me I couldn't stay I was planning to sit across the street, with all my bags, and wait, in order to show them that I was desperate, that I was ready and that I wanted to change. I was beyond grateful when they allowed me to stay!

The next few weeks were difficult for me. I wanted to change, my mind was made up that I wasn't leaving, but I constantly struggled with the guilt and the shame of my actions. Reality had hit me hard. I realized the pain and hurt that I had caused my wife, my daughter and my loved ones. I could not help but ask myself the question, "What happened? How did I get to this point?" I was determined to never go back to that old life again. It was during those months that I surrendered my life to Jesus Christ not just as my Savior but also as my Lord.

As I went through the program, God began to restore

my mind, my health and my relationship with my beloved wife. There was one day I got a phone call from my wife and she had just heard some very upsetting news about some things I had done during my addiction. She had also recently watched a 60 Minutes episode on meth use. She was terribly afraid that I would go back to meth. She asked me, "How do I know that you are really going to change?" That conversation has always stayed with me. I went to the Brockton Teen Challenge altar and on my knees and prayed, "God, please don't give me my family back if I am going to use drugs again." After that day, my relationship with Christ grew stronger and God began His miracle work of restoring my family from my devastating addiction.

> When everyone else would have given up,
> God stepped in and came to my rescue!

I progressed through the program, slowly but surely, with my share of issues and struggles, but I never gave up on God. He did what I could not do. He miraculously set me free, restored my family and gave me a new life in Christ!

My wife and daughter came to visit while I was in the program and our wonderful relationship began again! My wife had her husband back, my daughter had her daddy back and my mother had her son back. I had a new life and relationship with my Heavenly Father for which I am forever thankful. I'm thankful for the dedicated staff at Teen Challenge who helped me through the process of change and never gave up on me.

Today, through the help of our Lord and Savior Jesus Christ and the life changing work of Teen Challenge, I have a new life. I am no longer bound by drugs, alcohol, shame, guilt or living an empty life. At one point, living a normal life was only a dream beyond my grasp, but I finished the program and my wife and daughter relocated to New England. A few years later, God blessed us with our son, Carter!

Today, I am thankful to be able to pick up my son and daughter from school, take them to the park, read to them and tuck them into bed at night. Today, I am able to go to their sports games and practices. I am there for them when they need to talk. I am able to be the dad I have always wanted to be.

After completing the program, I stayed on for the internship program and never left. I became dedicated to the mission of Teen Challenge, helping others who were once bound in addiction to experience the hope and freedom that our Lord and Savior, Jesus Christ gives.

Since 2006, my wife and I have served the brokenhearted alongside Teen Challenge New England and our lives have never been the same. Today, I continue to serve Teen Challenge as the Director of the Brockton Campus and find great joy in seeing men set free from addiction through the love of Christ. My wife, Allie, loves Teen Challenge and is forever grateful for Teen Challenge being there when she bought me the one-way ticket to Boston! She has served at Teen Challenge since 2006. She is passionate about missions and reaches out to many broken, addicted people on the streets and to children and families, with the love and compassion of Christ.Our children Kylie and Carter have grown up in the ministry of Teen Challenge.

Far too many fatherless young men come through our doors at Teen Challenge, abandoned and hurting convinced that nothing but drugs and alcohol could possibly ease their pain. That was me, but I have come to know a Father whose love fills every void, whose grace erases the past, whose power transforms the future. God's love took me off the list of the fatherless. I'm thankful for God's lifesaving power through Jesus Christ and for his keeping power. My life once could have been considered beyond hope, but because the scripture found in Matthew 19:26 is true: "With God all things are possible." I now have a "Changed Life!"

Chapter 11
A Changed Life

Jacqueline Strothoff

"God, help me!" I screamed, as I held the lifeless body of my younger brother in my arms. It was more a cry of desperation than a prayer. I didn't have a relationship with God.

I had just injected cocaine into my own arm to be sure the drug was okay before giving it to Roger. I gave my brother an injection and within minutes his body began to convulse. I knelt down on the floor and gathered him into my arms. Minutes later, as I held him, he died. He was only 19 years old.

I couldn't believe what was happening. I had overdosed on cocaine before and sometimes I would convulse, but afterwards I would regain consciousness. But now, my brother laid motionless, his lips already turning blue.

Thinking he needed oxygen I dragged his body out onto the balcony of my apartment. I desperately tried breathing into him, but he wouldn't respond. I kept yelling at him to breathe, but there was no movement. Frantically, I started screaming up into the night sky, "God help me!"

Shortly thereafter, some men in white jackets arrived along with some police officers. Someone had called for help. They pried my brother out of my arms and strapped me to an ambulance cot. I was admitted to the psychiatric ward of a local hospital. My brother's body was taken to another hospital.

I dearly loved my little brother, as did anyone who knew him. He continued to look up to me regardless of the things I had done or who I had become.

> I tried to shield him from my sordid lifestyle as much as I could, but now he was gone and his death was a result of my actions.

It was one more part of a nightmare that had been going on since I was 14 years old. I was 26 years old and I wondered when it would ever end.

But Let Me Go Back To The Beginning

Born in Pittsburgh, Pennsylvania, I was the oldest of six children. My parents were good people, we lived in a nice home in the suburbs, and my childhood was "normal." There had been some incidents of sexual abuse in my early childhood by a distant relative and a neighborhood boy, but I didn't have a clear memory of it at the time nor had I ever connected it to the emptiness and pain I felt inside.

When I was 12 years old my family moved to Maryland, just outside Washington, D.C. While attending junior high school, I began to hang around with those considered to be "the wrong crowd." We would smoke, drink alcohol, and take pills.

The feelings I would get from using those substances made me feel peaceful and happy inside. The problem was, those feelings never lasted. In addition to the drug and alcohol use, I became sexually promiscuous and more rebellious. Because of these things, my academic performance began to fail.

At the age of 14, I tried to commit suicide for the first time. My steady boyfriend had just broken up with me and as an adolescent I felt as though it was the end of my world. I reacted by slicing my wrist with a razor blade.

One day I met a guy who was idolized by some of my friends. He was much older than me but I was flattered by his attention and the popularity it brought me. When I was barely 16 years old, I became pregnant by him, dropped out of school and got married. It wasn't long before I discovered he wasn't the man I thought he was. He would beat me at the slightest provocation or for no reason at all. I always walked on eggshells and lived in fear. I didn't know how to cope with the violence, but assumed it was my fault. Shame, guilt and fear caused me to keep the abuse a secret.

In my sixth month of pregnancy, he had beaten me so badly I began hemorrhaging and was rushed to the hospital. The baby was stillborn. A few days later, it was discovered I had been pregnant with twins. They had to surgically remove the other dead baby. I was declared sterile due to the infection that had developed. As a result, my parents sent me to Pittsburgh to live with my grandparents. At the time I was battling anxiety and nightmares. I found a connection at school for barbiturates and I was off and running again. The lifestyle of drugs, alcohol, and sexual behavior increased to a new level.

In the fall of 1966, I entered Penn State University, and I looked forward to a fresh start, but once again, I was drawn to the wrong crowd of people and my love affair with heroin began. The first time someone injected it into my arm, I knew I had found what I had been looking for all my life. The peace and feeling of euphoria was incredible and the pain was gone! But that peace was a lie and a cheap imitation offered by the devil. The pain that was hidden beneath this false pool of peace was far greater than anything I had ever imagined. By the end of that summer in Wildwood, New Jersey, my 17 year old life had become drug infested. Every single day found me high on something. My deceived mind thought, "This is really the life".

Nobody ever really intends to become a heroin addict.

We don't wake up one morning and say "Gee, I think I'd like to become a junkie when I grow up." Even in the early stages of using you tell yourself you will manage to do what none of the others could. You believe the lie that you will be able to control the monster. After thinking I was in control of my drug use, one day that monster turned on me. My life was consumed by getting high. All my time, money and energy were directed toward chasing bags of dope. Things that used to frighten me, became ordinary. I became a con artist and seasoned liar. Stealing progressed from petty larceny to armed robbery. The world of prostitution, sexual assault, and physical abuse became real. Arrests were happening more frequently as well as jail time. As the violence in my world increased, I began to carry a gun. Waking up in psychiatric wards or strange places after overdoses was common. It all seemed so surreal. How did this happen to me?

The first time I ever tried to stop using heroin, it was due to an accident. My grandparents planned a silver wedding anniversary for my parents in Pittsburgh, Pennsylvania. I was living in Florida at the time with a drug dealer. I agreed to fly up for the weekend and packaged enough heroin for the trip. When we arrived home from the airport, I went to the bathroom to shoot up and realized the drugs were gone. I became panic stricken. Sneaking out of my grandmother's house that night, I headed for Shadyside to try and find some dope but all I could get were barbiturates. They helped me sleep that night, but I awoke sick the next morning. Deciding my only hope was to get a dose of methadone from a sympathetic doctor, I went to St. Francis Hospital. The doctor refused me methadone, but suggested I talk to their drug counselor. Waiting for him in the emergency room, I became sicker. Finally, I slipped a syringe off a medical cart, went into the restroom and shot up the barbiturates.

When they unlocked the restroom door, they found me slumped over the toilet with the needle still in my arm. My lips were blue and they thought I was dead.

Waking up in the emergency room with IV's in my arms, the first face that I saw was my father's brother, crying. Uncle Bob had been the only one left at my grandmother's house when the call came from the hospital. The story of how we tracked some heroin was beyond belief, but I had to get my fix before we went to the party. After everyone else had left, we told my parents the truth. The next morning I woke up with the awareness that my father was standing in the doorway of the bedroom. When he realized I was awake, he crossed the room, knelt down beside my bed, and began to cry. I was devastated because I had never seen my father cry before. He pleaded with me to get help and I agreed to go back home with them to

Virginia to find a program. If the first part of my nightmare was living the life of a junkie, then the second part had to be trying to get free from that life!

The Challenge Had Just Begun!

There was a drug detoxification program in a hospital near their home. While in treatment, I was visited by a Federal Marshal for outstanding warrants. Upon my release I was taken to a hearing in Alexandria, Virginia and the judge ordered me to treatment at the government program in Lexington, Kentucky, simply known as "The Cure." In a matter of weeks I was thrown out for using drugs there. I moved back to Philadelphia, quickly found my old junkie friends and jumped right back into the life. At a time when the heroin supply became scarce, I studied the Physician's Desk Reference books at the library until I could pass as a pharmacist's assistant. I fabricated resumes and listing out of state references gave me enough time to get hired, empty the narcotics cabinets, and hit the streets before anyone realized what happened.

Since the pharmaceutical drugs were pure, my boyfriend, Michael and I were badly strung-out and overdosing on a regular basis. On the evening of November 1, 1972, I returned home with another friend. We discovered Michael unconscious in the bathtub. We figured he had just done too much dope and pulled him out of the tub and onto the waterbed. He was still breathing. We continued packaging dope and getting high through the night. I lay down beside him in the wee hours of the morning and fell asleep. Around 6:00 in the morning, I woke up freezing cold and quickly realized it was because he was so cold. He was lying motionless, his lips were blue, there was white foam around his mouth and he wasn't breathing. He was dead. Feeling as if I were in a trance, I walked to the corner payphone and called my friend that had been with me the night before. "You need to come over right away", I said. When he arrived, he went into the bedroom and then returned, confirming what I already knew to be true. We shot up and then went for a ride to talk about what we were going to do. Calling the authorities was out of the question. I reasoned that if the police came they would confiscate the drugs and send us to prison. Nothing would bring him back to life. We decided to bury him ourselves!

My friend had been employed at the time with a construction crew and had access to a bulldozer. We waited until Sunday to dig the grave. By the time we went back to retrieve the body he no longer looked human. The image was horrifying and the stench repulsive. We wrapped his body in a blue rug, dragged him down three flights of stairs, and pulled him up on the bed of a pick-up truck. We drove across the river to New Jersey where the job site was, and buried him. It was so hard for me to believe that drugs were more important to me than a human life. This was the life of someone that I loved dearly. How had I become so cold and calloused? What kind of animal had I become?

Life became increasingly difficult for me to manage and I began having serious mental problems. A friend called my father and alerted him of my condition. My dad paid to send me back to my grandparents in Pittsburgh, who admitted me to a psychiatric hospital. They later sent me to another drug program in Virginia, a therapeutic community. In a counseling session, I mentioned what happened with my boyfriend and the next thing I knew, I was being extradited to New Jersey. At the hearing, the judge found me guilty of "illegal disposition of a dead body", stipulated me to finish the program and gave me years of probation. Soon after that, I ran away from the program and hit the streets again. There hadn't been a "cure" but I was becoming more desperate to find one. Over the next several months, I would participate in hospital day treatment programs, primal therapy, residential 12 step programs, methadone programs, meetings and support groups. After exhausting every treatment option there was available, the frightening conclusion was this – I WAS STILL A JUNKIE!

Believing there was no escape from the hell I had created for myself, despising the things I had to do for my habit, and hating who I had become, I tried to commit suicide once again. Waking up in the emergency room, I began to cry as

I realized I had failed. My father was in the room and walked over to me. All I said was "Will you take me to the clinic to get my methadone or not?" They hadn't even taken the tubes out of me yet, but all I could think of was getting drugs.

It was on December 7, 1974, the night my brother Roger had died from the injection I had given him.

> That night I was placed in an isolation room, strapped down to the bed with an attendant by my side.

They began detoxing me and the feeling of hopelessness was beyond words, I knew my life was over.

While I was in this condition, God sent a man to me. Frank Marcello was one of my father's best friends from Pittsburgh. He was the artist who designed the book jacket for "Please Make Me Cry", a testimony of a woman whose life had been similar to mine, however Jesus Christ had changed her life. Now Frank had come to me, against all odds, with the same message. With tears streaming down his cheeks, and my father standing by his side, he looked into my eyes and said, "God has sent me here to tell you that if you will surrender your life to Him, He will change you and use you to help others and glorify His name." I just stared at him trying to understand what he was saying. "Jacqui," he asked, "will you pray with me and give your life to Jesus?" Now tears were streaming down my face as I nodded yes. Nothing visibly happened during or after the prayer, but the truth was that everything happened. When I asked Jesus to forgive my sins, cleanse my heart, and come live in me, He did, whether I could feel it or not.

It was the day of my brother's funeral. After I had been detoxed, I was transferred to a mental hospital in Fairfax, Virginia. I was taken to a hearing in shackles before a panel that made the decision to sentence me to an institution for the criminally insane. My criminal record and history caused them to believe I was a danger to others and myself. My father was present at this time when the decision was read. I could barely look at him, it was so painful. While I was waiting for transfer, I read the book "Please Make Me Cry", that Frank had given me. I thought either this woman is the biggest liar, or this is the greatest news I have ever heard. I longed for what God had done for her and asked God if he was able to do the same thing for me. Shortly after that prayer, I was discharged from the hospital without explanation. They gave me a taxi voucher for wherever I wanted to go and a brown paper grocery bag containing all that I owned. The problem was, I had no place to go. So I headed back to the streets and the only life I knew.

One February night I was sleeping on newspapers in an empty apartment without heat. I still had the book and on the back was printed, "If You Need Help Call This Number", so I walked to a phone booth and made a collect call to the program. They paid for a bus ticket to get me to the program. It was February 1975 when I arrived there in York, Pennsylvania. They put me to bed because I was high. Waking up the next morning, I looked out the window beside the bottom bunk where I had slept and all I could see were trees! So I started to feel under the bunk to find my shoes. I didn't know what I had done coming here, but I knew I would be getting sick soon and wanted to get back to the city.

Suddenly, there was the director, rejecting all my reasons to leave. She made me a proposition. "If you will let us pray for you and stay for 24 hours, then we will put you on a bus back to D.C." She had a deal. I could do anything for 24 hours. She and the girls laid hands on me (which freaked me out and I kept my eyes open) and began to pray. Almost immediately, it was as if a fire ignited in my belly. It began to radiate throughout my whole body. "What is this", I cried, "I feel like I am on fire!" They said it was God touching me and healing me. Afterward, there was never a trace of sickness from withdrawl. I had a huge appetite. I slept like a baby that night. God had my full attention. A couple days later in chapel, the director's husband was preaching and asked those of us that were new to stand up and thank God for the new life He had given us. So I did as I was asked, raised my hands and began to thank Him, when suddenly I felt completely overwhelmed by the Holy Spirit.

God's love seemed to sweep over me in waves. It was as if the fire of His love was burning all the sin, shame, and guilt that I carried, right out of me. Unclean feelings I had about myself were being washed away by continual waves of His mercy and forgiveness. Although I couldn't comprehend what was happening to me, I knew it was unlike anything I had ever experienced in my life before. A few hours later, when I finally stood up, I knew beyond any shadow of a doubt, that I would never be the same. Whatever just happened had changed me from the inside out. It had touched the deepest part of me. I felt as if I was a brand new person. What was this?

The staff began to share with me from God's word explaining more fully what it meant to be spiritually re-born and have a personal relationship with Jesus Christ. What seemed most awesome to me was the fact that He died for me before I ever heard of Him. While I was still a very bad person, He extended His love to me. So many others had withheld their love until I could clean myself up and get my act together. Jesus knew I could never do that alone. Loving me first, He offered the only thing that could clean me up – His own precious blood shed 2,000 years ago for all mankind. But even without my understanding, God's amazing love captured my heart.

My hunger to know God was great. There were many struggles in my life as I was going through the program, but the things I used to live for no longer held any attraction for me. From the beginning, I knew one day I would be working with women who were bound by the same kinds of sin that I had been. A man of God by the name of David Wilkerson had established a school of ministry called Twin Oaks Leadership Academy. It was designed to equip and train graduates of discipleship ministries who felt called to work with people who had life controlling problems. That was me!

Those of us who were chosen arrived at Twin Oaks in Lindale, Texas, on a hot summer day in June 1976. My year at that school was the best year of my life. Once again there were Bible classes, prayer times, great church services with some famous guest speakers, and evangelistic outreaches in places like Fort Lauderdale and New York City. My love for and devotion to Jesus increased daily and our relationship grew deeper and deeper as the months flew by. After commencement we were required to complete a one-year internship in a ministry related to our calling. I was invited to go to Southern California Teen Challenge in Riverside, California.

On November 11, 1977, I had just finished watching a program about abused women. I closed my eyes, bowed my head and wept quietly to myself, as I asked God why there were not more places for these women to go for help. Suddenly, with my eyes still closed, it was if I was watching a movie of a large home that God was describing to me as a spiritual hospital. It was filled with women who had all manner of problems, but they were all being changed and healed in His presence. It was thrilling! I thought this would all fall into place within a few months or so. When it didn't happen that way I became discouraged, but I never could forget what I had seen and heard.

In Arlington, Virginia, on February 17, 1979, Robert Strothoff and I were married. His former life had been like my own, and the desire of his heart was to reach other men for Christ who were bound by the same kind of addictions he had. Since neither of us were able to have children, we thought God must have considered this when He brought us together. However, God gave us a gift on our first wedding anniversary. It was on that day I discovered that I was pregnant with my son, Justin. Six years later, I was waiting to have a hysterectomy when I discovered that I was pregnant with my daughter, Chelsea. The Lord had healed me!

During the summer of 1988, we move to Rhode Island. My husband was asked to begin a discipleship ministry in Providence to complement the existing one in Boston, called Outreach Ministries.

A few years later, my vision from 1977 became a reality. God used my clinical experience, treating sexually abused victims, combined with my biblical knowledge, to enable me to minister to women living as I used to. Now, it's been 20

Changed Lives

years of seeing "changed lives." I am the executive director of the Teen Challenge for Women in Providence, Rhode Island. A building that was once a funeral home is now a place that celebrates new life.

Currently God is expanding my vision beyond our current adult women's program. I believe God will provide a property for us that will increase our capacity to 100 residents. In addition to the adult women, we want to include adolescents and children. It will be a campus that offers help and restoration for whole families. Please pray with us for the dream to become a reality. Remember, "With God all things are possible ". (Matthew 19:26)

I have been enjoying my "Changed Life." It has been 40 years since I first accepted Jesus Christ as my personal Savior and was set free from addiction and a destructive lifestyle. How about you? Are you ready for the One who created you to change you into who you were meant to be?

Chapter 12
Drug Prevention for Parents

Allison Cruz

There are more than 1,200 Teen Challenge programs around the world. According to the United Nations, there are more than 250 million people worldwide struggling with drug abuse. At Teen Challenge, we are committed to doing everything we can to reach people with life controlling problems around the globe, and it all starts with prevention.

Through the years, we have received thousands of heartbreaking calls from parents in need of hope and help for their children. One father who lost his young son from a drug overdose said, "If I had spoken to you just two weeks earlier, I might not have buried my son." His grief-filled words will remain in our hearts for years to come as they echo the resounding cry for drug prevention programs in the lives of young people.

Teen Challenge sees this devastation first-hand and

wants to bring drug prevention. As Benjamin Franklin said, "An ounce of prevention is worth a pound of cure." For more than 50 years, Teen Challenge New England and New Jersey has helped thousands of men, women and youth find freedom from addiction, and we rejoice in their miraculously changed lives; however, prevention is a far better tool than intervention. We want to prevent children and teens from drug and alcohol abuse by equipping parents.

According to CASA Columbia, "Each year federal, state and local governments spend close to $500 billion on addiction and risky substance use, but for every dollar that federal and state governments spend, only two cents goes to prevention and treatment." "More than 90% of people with addiction problems began smoking, drinking or using other drugs before age 18."

The tendency is to think, "Addiction can never happen to my child" and while we wish that were true, addiction knows no bounds. Drug addiction and alcoholism can happen to anyone. It affects all social, ethnic and economic backgrounds and it is our goal to prevent it.

Tips For Drug Prevention For Parents
1. Lock up your prescription medications
Countless young people start experimenting with drugs from their parents' medicine cabinet. Locking up your

prescription medications cannot be stressed strongly enough. Trying pills just one time can begin a lifetime of addiction.

2. Consider drug testing your kids at home

This can be an effective tool to combat peer pressure. When asked to use illegal substances, your children can tell their friends they can't because they are drug screened at home.

3. Talk to your children early and often

Tell your children you want them to be drug free. Have age appropriate conversations about the dangers of experimenting with drug and alcohol use. Capture every opportunity to alert them to potential dangers in their environment. Teach them to think freely and act independently and not to do something because everyone else is doing it. This type of clear communication with your children helps them avoid negative peer pressure. Role-playing of specific situations is one way to help your child know just what to say. Help them to develop making good decisions. Most of all, tell your children often that you love them. Children who know they are loved are less likely to disappoint those who love them. Pay attention not only to what you say but how you say it as well.

4. Know where your children are going and with whom

Get to know their friends and their parents so you will

be familiar with their activities. Make your own home open and available to your children's friends. Remember older children need parental supervision as much as younger children. Accept your role as the parent; don't try to be their friend.

5. Make quality family time a top priority

Spend time with your children even when they become teens. Decide how you can make high quality, enjoyable family time a habit. Little things make a difference; play board games, sports and do other activities together. This will show your children and teens that you care and it builds their self-confidence, which helps insulate them from risky behaviors. Children who feel good about themselves are less likely to deviate from what they know is right.

6. Have family dinners

According to the CASA report at Columbia University, "Kids who eat three or more meals weekly with their parents are less likely to use drugs," and "Eating family dinners at least five times a week drastically lowers a teen's chance of smoking, drinking and using drugs." This report also said, "Teens who have fewer than three family dinners a week are 3.5 times more likely to have abused prescription drugs and to have used illegal drugs other than marijuana, three times more likely to have used marijuana, more than 2.5 more likely to have smoked cigarettes, and 1.5 times more likely to have tried alcohol." So the more often you have dinner together, the more you prevent drug addiction. Therefore, make dinner a special family time. Turn off phones and electronics and enjoy the company of your family members. Especially use this time to try to connect and not to criticize, complain or argue.

7. Listen and share life

"An average parent spends 38.5 minutes per week in meaningful conversation with their kids." Meaningful conversations build healthy family relationships. Learn to actively listen to your kids. Show them love in a variety of ways and be sure to communicate with them daily. Demonstrate your respect and sincerity towards them. Ask them questions about what they are interested in. If you are busy and cannot be interrupted, tell them and prioritize a time to talk immediately after finishing - then do it. Few things should get in the way of listening to our kids when they want our attention. Focus on what "good things" you want to develop within your child. Spend time together as a family and individually with each child to develop strong bonds of love. Show plenty of affection often and in hugs and kisses, even when they grow older. Communicate encouragement and affirmation by word and deed. (high-fives, thumbs-up, winks, "that's my guy", "you go girl", "I knew you could do it", etc.)

8. Do not ignore the red flags

Do not dismiss changes in behavior as "normal" teenage behavior. Don't be afraid to ask for help. Don't fall prey to the "not my kid" syndrome; remember addiction can happen to anyone. Regardless of society's attitudes toward marijuana use and its decriminalization, a child who uses marijuana is more vulnerable to other risky behaviors. The fact remains that young people who begin to use illegal drugs are more at risk because their brains are not yet fully developed until they are over 20 years old. According to the National Institute on Drug abuse, "studies of high school students and their patterns of drug use shows that very few young people use other drugs without first trying marijuana. One of the reasons is smoking marijuana puts teens in touch with those who sell drugs- all types. Long-term studies of high school aged teens show patterns of drug use, that most teenagers who use other drugs have smoked marijuana, drank alcohol or used tobacco first." Also, "Teens who use drugs are five more times likely to have sex than teens who do not use drugs," according to the National Center on Addiction and Substance Abuse at Columbia University. Teens have been known to start experimenting by the age of thirteen or younger and some teens can hide it from their parents for more than two years. Also, avoid use of prescription or over-the-counter medicines as a quick fix for pain, which may send the wrong message that is so prevalent in the media, that chemicals are the cure for all discomfort. Be cognizant that your use of alcohol may also influence your children. Don't use excuses like "I had a rough day." Your children will likely follow your lead. It is better to discuss issues of stress and conflict together; to teach them that such struggles are a normal part of life. Show them you can cope without drugs and alcohol.

9. Shared values

Be a living example of what you want your kids to be in words and actions. Never give the message to your children that it's okay to be dishonest when convenient. Clarify family rules and discuss the consequences of breaking them. Young people are less inclined to use tobacco, alcohol or drugs when parents set clear rules prohibiting their use and live that life before their children. Probably the greatest value parents and grandparents can share with their kids is a personal, vibrant faith in God. Getting involved with a local church that has a youth group can be a positive outlet for your teen. Yet even young people who attend church are not immune from trouble. Research shows that those who indicate a personal faith in God, participate in church and other extracurricular activities, are less likely to indulge themselves in drugs or alcohol. Parents, you can provide good models for your children by what you do and what you avoid doing.

Warning Signs That You Child
May Be Using Drugs or Alcohol

When children begin using drugs, they usually exhibit many different signs which parents need to watch out for. Unfortunately, many parents often write-off these signs as normal adolescent behavior and as a result they don't realize that their child is into drugs until it is too late. How can you as a parent know for sure whether or not your child is in danger of falling into drugs? Simply! By understanding that every child is in danger of this. The parent who says "not my kid," is the same parent who will miss all the signs that their child has started experimenting with drugs. Often parents stay in this state of denial until their son or daughter is arrested or overdoses, and by then it is too late. So what should you as parents be looking for as signs that your child is experimenting with drugs or alcohol?

1. Dramatic changes in style of clothes, hair, and music

These outward signs of rebellion should be obvious to a parent. Has your child started listening to radically different music such as heavy metal or punk rock? Is your child coloring their hair just to fit in? Is your child dressing down to fit in with friends at school? All of these are outward signs that your child is succumbing to peer pressure and all these should serve as warning signs to you that your child is in danger of falling into the same kind of peer pressure when it comes to drugs.

2. Hanging out with the wrong crowd

Your child might try and tell you that their friends are cool kids. But you need to take a close look at the kinds of kids your child is hanging out with. Chances are the way these friends behave is the way your child behaves when you're not around. Do some of your child's friends smoke cigarettes? If so, odds are your child is smoking too. Your child's friends are like a mirror for your son or daughter -- they look at themselves in that mirror and try to conform to what they see there.

3. Tardiness and/or truancies

Take the initiative to stay in touch with your child's school about their attendance record. Never assume that their school will be in touch with you if there is a problem. If your child is getting into drugs, odds are they will start skipping class from time to time. They may take off during the middle of school. Realize kids are great at covering up their behavior and most know how to forge their parent's signature.

4. Isolating from family

Does your child act distant? When you ask what they have been up to, do they give some vague reply? Do they want to eat in their room instead of with the family? Children know that the easiest lie to tell is the one they can avoid having to tell. Isolation and poor communication may signify your child is hiding something.

5. Changes in attitude and personality

Has your child suddenly got a new personality that you don't appreciate? Have they developed a tough guy/girl attitude? These kinds of attitude changes can be a sign of drug experimentation. You may think it is normal teenage behavior but don't make that mistake because you may overlook one of the most obvious signs of a drug problem.

6. Change in sleep patterns

This sign is fairly obvious; staying up late (or even all night) frequently and refusing to get up in the morning. Sleeping far too much or too little is a side effect of stimulant abuse.

7. Bad language

Excessive use of foul or obscene language may indicate that your child is giving into peer pressure. Let this act as a warning sign to you that future peer pressure to use drugs may not be far away.

8. Eating way too much or way too little

This obvious sign is often overlooked as normal teenage behavior. Smoking marijuana can cause your child to come home ravenous and devour almost everything in the refrigerator. On the other hand if your child skips a lot of meals and is losing weight, it may be indicative of amphetamine abuse.

9. Paranoia - everyone is out to get them

Treating others as the enemy or thinking that everybody is out to get you is paranoia. This is not normal behavior and is a very common sign of drug abuse that you don't have to look far to see.

10. Dilated eyes - red eyes - glazed eyes

Do your child's eyes look funny? If their pupils are very large or small, or glazed looking, or the whites are red; this may be a sign of drug abuse. Some may even wear sunglasses all the time to cover up, while saying they are just trying to look cool.

11. Sudden bursts of anger

A child that has developed a violent side such as being prone to sudden, uncontrollable fits of anger may be using drugs. This is not just physical violence (though that is often the case) but can also be one who is always yelling at and/or threatening others.

12. Lies

Drug abuse requires lots of lying to cover up. If you

wonder whether your child is telling you the truth or not, there is a good chance that your instincts are correct. Be persistent to learn what it is that they are covering up.

13. Dramatic mood swings

Very happy and 'up' one day and then completely depressed and 'down' the next day is often confused with 'normal' teenage behavior, but it can be a sign of drug abuse.

14. Excessive money spending or money disappearing

Drugs cost money. If your child keeps telling you he needs money or if money is continually missing from your home, it's time to have a serious talk. Round amounts like twenty or fifty dollars are common amounts needed for drugs.

What To Do When You Know There Is A Problem

If you know for sure that your child is experimenting with drugs and alcohol, what you do next is a matter of utmost importance. Some parents shrug drug experimentation off as a phase a child goes through as they grow up. Other parents just want to deny the problem and hope it will go away on its own. But the truth is you can't ignore your child's drug problem; it will not go away on its own, it will only get worse! Here are some suggestions on what you can do:

• Find out what kinds of drugs are being used. Often

children will claim they are only smoking marijuana when they are really using other drugs also. Take the time to investigate matters for yourself, and find out what's really going on.

• Begin to scrutinize your child's choice of friends. If your son or daughter is experimenting with drugs, some of their friends are also involved. It is important to find out which of these friends are involved in this experimentation and get your child away from these influences. This is one of the most difficult things to accomplish, but it is also one of the most necessary. Bad friends corrupt good morals. Of those that leave Teen Challenge and end up back on drugs, one of the most common reasons is that they went back to the same old friends and environment where they used drugs before. Those that stay clean invariably find a new set of friends that encourage and support good values and wholesome fun that does not include drugs and alcohol.

• Get your kids involved in a good church and its activities. It is very important not only to get your children away from kids who are bad influences on them, but to get them around people who will have a positive impact on their life. Churches center many of their activities around family and are often overlooked as a source for help. Students who have completed the Teen Challenge program and continue to stay off drugs often cite church activities as one reason that they are able to "stay clean."

• Get involved in your kid's life. Today's fast-paced world has taken its toll on parenting. Many parents have the idea that spending time with their children is watching television with them. That is not the kind of involvement your child needs! Spend quality time with your son or daughter, helping with homework or just sit down each day and talk about what your child did that day. Also take the time to personally attend their activities with them. Show your children that you care about them by doing things with them. This also gives you an opportunity to see who their friends are and how they act when they are together.

• Set standards for your child. Let them know what you expect of them around the house, what their chores are and the consequences for not doing them. Also set standards for your child at school. Tell your children what kind of grades you expect them to achieve. And finally, give them standards for behavior. Your child needs to know that using drugs and alcohol is unacceptable behavior. Don't be afraid to deal with your child using tough love if he or she continues to experiment with drugs or alcohol. The alternatives are much worse!

• Seek help from people who understand what you are going through. The youth pastor at the church your family attends is one person you can talk to about what your child is going through.

• Teen Challenge is another alternative for help.

Teen Challenge has been helping people
in New England for over 50 years

Contact the Teen Challenge center nearest you for help with your son or daughter's drug or alcohol problem and referrals to local support groups and resources. It is very important for you to remember that you are not alone!

Suggested Readings for Parents, Juveniles and Teens

- Boundaries with Kids by Henry Cloud and John Townsend
- Search for Significance (student edition) by Robert McGee
- Bringing Up Boys by James Dobson
- When Good Kids Make Bad Choices by Elyse Fitzpatrick
- How to be a Happy, Healthy Family by Jim Burns
- Relational Parenting by Ross Campbell
- On Becoming Teen Wise by Ezzo and Buckman
- The Seven Cries of Today's Teens by Timothy Smith
- The Bondage Breaker (youth edition) by Neil Anderson
- Every Young Man's Battle by Stephen Arterburn
- Not Guilty by Jim and Barbara Dycus
- The Wounded Spirit by Frank Peretti
- Turning Hurts into Halos by Robert Schuller
- The Five Love Languages of Teenagers by Gary Chapman
- Mercy for Eating Disorders by Nancy Alcorn

Works Cited

1. Nancy Leedberg, Community Education Officer, Brockton Police Department.
2. CASAColumbia. "Addiction by the numbers". <http:// www.casacolumbia.org. Accessed May 2014. Accessed May 2014.
3. CASAColumbia. <http:// www.casacolumbia.org/addiction-prevention/teenage-addiction>. Accessed May 2014.
4. Teen Challenge Southeast Region. http://www.teenchallenge.cc/plaintext/home/home.aspx. Accessed June 2014.

Make a Difference!

1. Raise Your Level of Awareness:
Get training to help with prevention and intervention in the lives of those struggling!

2. Outreach In Your Local Community:
Bring hope by joining an experienced group doing outreach in your community, and reach out to those struggling with addiction, alcoholism and life controlling problems.

3. Become a Volunteer:
Contact the Adult and Teen Challenge Center nearest you for volunteer opportunities!

4. The Hope Line:
Share the Teen Challenge HOPE line: 1-855-404-HOPE with someone you know that is struggling with addiction.

5. Prayer:
Pray for people to be set free from addiction and alcoholism, pray for the students, thier families, and staff in our Teen Challenge homes.

$1-A-DAY
Sponsor-A-Student Campaign

An Investment in Lives that Pays Eternal Dividends

As a sponsor, you can be a lifeline of encouragement and support to an addicted young person who is discovering God's love and a new life at Teen Challenge.

For just $1 a day/$30 a month, you can help underwrite the cost of a student in the residential, recovery program and give a young man or woman in our homes real hope for a promising future without drugs or alcohol addiction!

Your partnership will be a tremendous encouragement to them as they are transformed by a loving God from the inside out and become loving, healthy members of their families and a credit to their communities as caring, responsible and productive citizens without dependence on drugs or alcohol.

Men and women who have lived wisely and well will shine
brilliantly, like the cloudless, star-strewn night skies.
And those who put others on the right path
to life will glow like stars forever.
Daniel 12:3, The Message

Call 508-586-1494 to see how you can become a $1-A-Day Sponsor!
Or visit our website: www.tcnewengland.org to pledge your support.

Thank you!

213

Schedule Teen Challenge

to come to your church, school or community event.

Contact the Teen Challenge Center nearest you today!

TEEN CHALLENGE
New England & New Jersey

Giving Hope to Addicts & Families

CHANGED LIVES

Ten True Stories: *From Addiction to Freedom*

Single Copy: $15

Case of 32: $350 - Free Shipping

eBook Download: $10

Get yours today at:

www.tcnewengland.org

**Stay tuned for
Changed Lives Vol. 2
Coming in 2015**

If you or someone you know is struggling with drug addiction, alcoholism or a life controlling problem, Teen Challenge is here to help.

Call the Teen Challenge HOPE Line at

1-855-404-HOPE

to speak to someone today and to get hope and help!

INVEST
IN A LIFE
BRING JOY
WITH JEWELRY

LET US HOST YOUR JEWELRY PARTY!
YOU INVITE YOUR FRIENDS...WE DO THE REST!
Partner with Teen Challenge and help change lives!

TEEN CHALLENGE WILL HOST YOUR JEWELRY
PARTY AT OUR WOMEN'S HOME IN PROVIDENCE,
RHODE ISLAND FOR A NIGHT FILLED WITH
MIRACULOUS STORIES OF CHANGED LIVES, AN
OPPORTUNITY TO MEET THE STAFF AND STUDENTS,
TOUR OUR HOME, AND PURCHASE HANDCRAFTED
JEWELRY OR DESIGN AND CREATE YOUR OWN.

Contact | jewelry@tcprovidence.org | 401-467-2970

HELP CHANGE A LIFE -
DONATE A VEHICLE TO TEEN CHALLENGE!

You can help change a life by donating your vehicle to Teen Challenge. Every car, truck, mini-van, boat, etc. we receive helps to fund the life-changing programs of Teen Challenge!

Donating your vehicle to Teen Challenge is simple.
Visit our website or call today!

www.tcnewengland.org | 508-586-1494
Help change a life!

Teen Challenge Catering
Breakfast • Lunch • Dinner • Weddings • Banque[t]
For more information, call 508-586-1494

Teen Challenge
Maintenance & Construction

Carpentry, Interior & Exterior Painting,
Tile/Hardwood Floors, Decks, Additions, Remodeling,
Clean Outs and More!
Call today for your free estimate!

Massachusetts
P: 508-586-1494
P: 508-341-8551

New Hampshire
P: 603-647-7770

Vermont
P: 802-635-7807

Corporate Headquarters
1315 Main Street
Brockton, MA 02301
P: 508-4084378
F: 508-580-4186
info@tcnewengland.org
www.tcnewengland.org

Brockton, MA Men's Campus
1315 Main Street
Brockton, MA 02301
P: 508-586-1494
F: 508-580-4186
director@tcbrockton.org
www.tcbrockton.org

Boston, MA Men's Campus
16 Bloomfield Street
Dorchester, MA 02124
P: 617-318-1380
F: 617-318-1385
director@tcboston.org
www.tcboston.org

Maine Men's Campus
11 Hudson Lane
Winthrop, ME 04364
P: 207-377-2801
F: 207-377-2806
director@tcmaine.org
www.tcmaine.org

New Hampshire Men's Campus
147 Laurel Street
Manchester, NH 03103
P: 603-647-7770
F: 603-647-7570
director@tcnewhampshire.org
www.tcnewhampshire.org

Rhode Island Women's Campus
572 Elmwood Avenue
Providence, RI 02907
P: 401-467-2970
F: 401-461-3510
director@tcrhodeisland.org
www.tcrhodeisland.org

Connecticut Men's Campus
86 Spring Street
New Haven, CT 06534
P: 203-789-6172
F: 203-789-1127
director@tcconnecticut.org
www.tcconnecticut.org

Vermont Men's Campus
1296 Collins Hill Road
Johnson, VT 05656
P: 802-635-7807
F: 802-635-7029
director@tcvermont.org
www.tcvermont.org

New Jersey Men's Campus
245 Stanton Mountain Road
Lebanon, NJ 08838
P: 973-374-2206
F: 973-374-5866
director@tcnewjersey.org
www.tcnewjersey.org

END ADDICTION
JOIN THE FIGHT AGAINST DRUG AND ALCOHOL ABUSE

Overdoses are on the rise,
addiction has become an epidemic.
Too many promising lives have been lost.

The **End Addiction** campaign will raise awareness
of this growing epidemic, help prevent young people
from going down the path of addiction and offer
HOPE to those trapped in addiction.

Addiction knows no bounds.
It affects people of all ages and from all walks of life.
If you or someone you know is struggling,
don't give up - change is possible!

Call the HOPE LINE today,

1-855-404-HOPE

Join the fight against drug and alcohol abuse
so that every addict will know that there is **HOPE**.

Do you have freedom?

Those struggling with drug and alcohol addiction are not free and desperately need the help of Jesus to save them, free them and restore them! If you don't know Jesus, you too, need the freedom from sin and the weight of the world.

Why do I need to know Jesus?

God created us to be in relationship with Him. Adam and Eve enjoyed a beautiful closeness with their Creator, but something tragic happened. They chose to disobey and rebel against God. This caused separation between God and man. All have sinned and fall short of the glory of God (Romans 3:23).

What does this mean for me?

God loves us so much that He sent His son, Jesus, to live a sinless life on earth, and then to die as a sacrifice for the sin that we deserve punishment for. Now our hearts can be made new and we can be reconciled back into a right relationship with God. This is VERY good news! Will you accept this free gift of salvation from your Father who loves you unrelentingly? (Romans 6:23) (John 3:16)

Where do I go from here?

To heaven when your life is over! Until then, walk with God, turn from sin, read the bible, get involved in church, talk with God regularly and tell people about this great news in your life.

"For Christ also suffered once for sins, the righteous for the unrighteous, that He might bring us to God." - 1 Peter 3:18 [ESV]